RUMORS AND BORDERS

Rumors and Borders

Eight Western Plays

By Red Shuttleworth

Humanitas Media Publishing

ACKNOWLEDGMENTS:

FAREWELL THE CATASTROPHE WORKS was first published in Alaska Quarterly Review.

THIS IS DEAD LEVEL was first published in Lucky 13 (University of Nevada Press, 1995)

The early drafts of these plays were written thanks to a 1989-1990 Nevada State Council on the Arts Playwriting Fellowship. I deeply appreciate this support and the encouragement of William L. Fox and Kirk Robertson.

Special Thanks to the late Jerry L. Crawford, Julie Jensen, and the late Davey Marlin-Jones, my teachers at University of Nevada, Las Vegas, for taking the time to read and reread these plays as they developed and for useful critiques. And Many Thanks, too, to Tom Loughlin at State University of New York at Fredonia and to Mike Barton at Drake University for advice and for being in my corner.

I am particularly grateful to the directors and actors who brought life to these plays, especially Maggie Winn-Jones, Toni Loppnow, and Gina Torrecilla.

Production histories can be found prior to each play.

For

Jessi Shuttleworth

Tom Loughlin

Paul Zarzyski

In Memoriam

Jerry L. Crawford

Contents

Days of Daring

Time: 1943

Locale: East of Tonopah, Nevada

Characters: CLOVER, 28
              BONNIE, 28, Clover's sister
              PADRE, 25, bounty hunter
              BERRY, 50, rancher

Days of Daring was first produced by University of Nevada, Las Vegas, on March 1, 1991. It was directed by Todd Espeland and Shawn Martin with the following cast:

Clover   Kim Danser
Bonnie   Gina Torrecilla
Padre   Danny Beaupre
Berry   Jim Henry

(A large backdrop painting of the country east of Tonopah, Nevada. A doorframe upstage, also a large window frame. Near the doorframe is an old hotel desk, beside which is a distressed couch. Somewhat downstage and off to one side is a metal frame bed, with a bedpan beside it. A heavy rope, like a church bell rope, hangs from above, almost at center stage, with enough slack for a coil. Lights up on CLOVER who is sitting on the bed, staring at a silent radio situated downstage on a wooden fruit crate. The lights flicker. CLOVER flinches, holds herself tight. She is in a tattered, late 1930's summer dress, and her hair is dirty. The lights go out. Lightning flash. As the lights come back on, there's a thunder clap. Rain hammers a tin roof. The rain eases off and stops. The lights flicker again. CLOVER rocks back and forth on the bed, arms crossed, hands gripping tight on upper arms. CLOVER stares at the radio. BONNIE enters, using a metal walker, for she has leg braces and can barely stay upright, but she is able to use the walker and, at the same time, propel forward a roller cart that has two tin cans on its tray (hot chocolate). With no small use of energy, BONNIE moves toward CLOVER. BONNIE is in a cowgirl blouse, cowhide skirt, and is barefoot like CLOVER.)

BONNIE: I put in extra. Like I promised yesterday. (*Pause.*) For a treat.

CLOVER: Hitler.

BONNIE: Drink up.

CLOVER: Hitler!

3

(*The lights flicker.*)

BONNIE: Summer storm.

CLOVER: Radio!

BONNIE: Not 'till you drink your cocoa.

CLOVER: Clover good girl.

BONNIE: Yes. Please pick up the drink.

(*Thunder clap.*)

CLOVER: God?

BONNIE: I told you. (*Pause.*) Clover, please, I can't keep standing.

(CLOVER *takes one of the cans and drinks from it.*)

BONNIE: That's better, isn't it?

(*The lights flicker.*)

CLOVER: Hitler. Spies!

(BONNIE *shuffles the walker to the rope, pulls on it and the rope moves upward until there is no coil, and, at the same time, a net cage, like a canopy, descends over* CLOVER *and her bed.*)

BONNIE: Night-night. (*She begins to shuffle to the couch.*)

CLOVER: (*Holding out her can.*) Not sweet.

BONNIE: It is sweet.

CLOVER: No!

BONNIE: There's an extra sugar cube in it.

CLOVER: Lie.

BONNIE: (*Now by the couch.*) Clover, today is Tuesday. You understand? (*No response.*) Berry won't bring more sugar for nearly a week. On his next trip to Tonopah.

CLOVER: Bonnie eat all sugar.

BONNIE: Go to sleep, Clover. Please.

(CLOVER *sits on her bed and rocks.* BONNIE *gets onto the couch with effort, lies down, pulls a* <u>Collier's</u> *magazine from beneath a cushion.*)

CLOVER: Clover pee-pee on bed?

BONNIE: (*Opening the magazine.*) Better <u>not</u>. Or you'll sleep on it for a week. (*She finds an article to read.*)

CLOVER: Read me? (*No response.*) Radio? Soft?

BONNIE: Get some sleep.

CLOVER: Read Hitler.

BONNIE: No.

CLOVER (Sings.) Ring, ring, ring.
             Goat butter gone.
             Ring, ring, ring,
             Sing goat butter gone.

BONNIE: (*Slaps her magazine on her leg.*) Go… to… sleep! Or else!

CLOVER: Ring, ring, ring,
        Loaf of bread.

BONNIE: Stop!

CLOVER: Ring, ring, ring,
        Farmer all dead.

(*Silence for a beat. Then lightning. The lights flicker.*)

CLOVER: Night Hitler! <u>Please</u>, radio!

(*Thunder clap.* CLOVER *rocks and constricts into a tight huddle.*)

BONNIE: Okay. If you're scared, sing <u>softly</u>.

CLOVER: <u>You </u>sing.

(BONNIE *rises from the couch with a grunt, gains her walker, and starts toward* CLOVER *with a rolled up* <u>Collier's</u> *clenched in one hand.*)

BONNIE: You are warned! Be good!

(*Thunder.* CLOVER *rocks.*)

CLOVER: Radio?

BONNIE: No! No radio. No singing. Just sleep. Sleep and dream. Dream pictures. (*Pause.*) Christ…. Dream red ice cream, blueberries…

CLOVER: Berry come?

BONNIE: <u>Blue</u>berries. (*She walks to the window, looks out, supported by the walker.*) Hellfire. (*She rushes, as best she can, to the rope.*)

CLOVER: Berry?

7

BONNIE: No. A stranger on a horse. (*She hauls on the rope to lift the canopy of netting off* CLOVER.)

CLOVER: Berry take me. Dust all over. In Berry Hudson.

BONNIE: Clover, it is <u>not</u> Berry. This is a stranger. Stay on your bed. <u>Stay</u>, Clover.

(PADRE *enters, carrying saddlebags and a canvas-over-burlap sack. He pauses as if adjusting to the dim light. A .30-30 rifle -with strap- is slung over his shoulder.* PADRE *is dressed in a dusty tan linen duster, open in front; striped dark trousers, faded purple shirt with a white cleric's collar; riding boots; and a broad-brim, low and rounded-crown Padre hat. Over the shirt is a metal breastplate with a President Cleveland treaty medal (large coin) on it. Around his neck and over a neck rag is a horse intestine canteen that is nearly empty.*)

BONNIE: Hello.

PADRE: (*Slight nod.*) Evening. (*He turns and walks to the old hotel desk. He places his saddlebags on the desk, uncoils the horse intestine canteen and puts it on the desk, too. He slaps the desk, looks around.*)

BONNIE: We can't help you.

PADRE: (*Pause as he stares at* BONNIE.) Does God take care of the oxen? That's from the good book. Should you do less?

CLOVER: No Berry.

PADRE: (*Nods to* CLOVER, *speaks to* BONNIE.) I need a room.

BONNIE: This is not a hotel anymore.

PADRE: I'll pay. Silver dollars.

BONNIE: No one's been upstairs to clean. There are no sheets.

PADRE: I have a bedroll.

BONNIE: Sorry… can't help you.

PADRE: Need water, too. (*He holds up his canteen.*) My horse is thirsty. (*To* CLOVER.) Bring him a bucket of water.

BONNIE: She can't. She'll…. Well, sir, she just can't.

PADRE: (*Takes out and stacks ten silver dollars.*) Miss, I just spent ten days on the Pancake Range. I need a bed… and water. This is where I need to have it. (*He looks at* CLOVER.) There's the money. (*Pause.*) Like it says in the Bible, Any sick among you? Call an elder of the church. And let him pray over her and anoint her with oil, in the Lord's name. (*Pause.*) I can do that. And more.

BONNIE: She doesn't need your help.

PADRE: And you? (*He walks to* BONNIE, *slowly reaching out his hand until the palm almost touches her forehead.*) Close your eyes, sister.

BONNIE: (*Scrunching backward.*) Please.

PADRE: (*Dropping his hand.*) Some's not ready. Okay… I'll go to my room upstairs. I take it I can choose the one I want. The ten silver dollars are yours. You can have two more when I come downstairs… come for the victuals you'll have for me. And for watering my horse. (*He starts to pick up his canteen and saddlebags.*)

BONNIE: This is a ghost town. No one stops here.

(*With a glance at* BONNIE, PADRE *exits, and we hear his weary steps on stairs long in disuse.*)

CLOVER: Man sleep here.

BONNIE: If he comes down, I'll…

CLOVER: Berry never sleeps.

BONNIE: Don't talk to him. (*She exits out the door.*)

CLOVER: (*Going to the radio.*) Sing, sing, sing,
Oh the buzzard she sing…

(CLOVER *turns on the radio and it squawks static. She turns the dial rapidly, too quickly to get a station. She hears* PADRE *coming down the stairs and backs off from the radio.* PADRE *enters.* CLOVER *backs toward her bed and squats and looks at him.* PADRE *has some sheets of paper and a few silver dollars. His rifle and breastplate are gone, replaced by a belly gun. Watching* CLOVER, *he places the money, papers, and his horse intestine canteen on the hotel desk. He slowly approaches her.*)

PADRE: Want something real bright? A silver dollar? I don't have any candy.

CLOVER: (*Points to the radio.*) Hitler.

PADRE: That right?

CLOVER: Hitler make radio fuzzy.

PADRE: (*Going to the radio.*) I'll turn it off. We can talk.

CLOVER: Radio sing 'n sing.

PADRE: You want a song?

CLOVER: (*Pause.*) Sing.

PADRE: "Blue-Eyed Elaine." You like that one?

CLOVER: Radio.

(PADRE *turns the radio dial and finds a station playing country music, maybe Ernest Tubb's "Walking the Floor Over You." For a moment they listen.*)

PADRE: Care to dance?

CLOVER: Can't dance.

(BONNIE *returns, goes to the radio and snaps it off.*)

BONNIE: Your horse is watered.

CLOVER: (*To* PADRE.) Dance?

BONNIE, Clover, go to bed.

PADRE: Don't send her away on my account. (*Pause.*) But I could use that food now. Then I'll put him out back.

BONNIE: Mister, if you sit the couch, I'll fetch food. And leave my sister be. She's not up to talking.)

(BONNIE *watches as* PADRE *goes to the couch and sits. Then she exits.*)

CLOVER: Ernest Topp?

PADRE: Once upon a time, in a hot dry land, there was this man. His daddy was the big king. And when his day came to die, all-longing for everybody's goodness…

CLOVER: Daddy died. Blood! (*She crosses her arms and rocks.*)

PADRE: (*He steps toward* CLOVER *to comfort her.*) Easy, easy girl. This king's son left his good works power to his elder helpers. (*From a few feet away, he offers his hand.*)

CLOVER: Clover good girl.

PADRE: (*Closer to her now.*) And through the hands of the king's son's helpers…

(BONNIE *enters, a paper sack in her mouth, like a retriever. She drops it.*)

BONNIE: Your food.

PADRE: (*Walks over, picks up the paper sack.*) Thank you.

BONNIE: (*As he pulls out two biscuits and a can of evaporated milk.*) There's a can opener behind the desk. That's all the food that's ready. (*Pause.*) I'll send breakfast with you. I rise early.

13

(PADRE *goes to the desk, adds two silver dollars to the stack of ten already there. He finds the can opener and opens the can. He takes a drink.*)

CLOVER: Radio.
(*As* PADRE *watches and eats a biscuit,* BONNIE *toes and shuffles the radio over to the bed. The radio is unsteady on the crate, but she gets it there without mishap.*)

BONNIE: Don't play the radio loud… and don't sing to it. (*She goes now to* PADRE.) Do you always invade… butt in? My sister is not well. I'm not well.

PADRE: The Lord takes me places.

BONNIE: The Lord's never been here. He don't know the way.

(PADRE *breaks off a piece of biscuit, holds it to* BONNIE'S *lips.*)

CLOVER: (*Turning up the volume and turning the dial to static.*) Only fuzz. Hitler fuzz.

PADRE: (*Holding a piece of biscuit to* BONNIE'S *lips.*) Body of Christ?

(BONNIE *shuffles the walker over to* CLOVER *and the radio.*)

14

BONNIE: Clover, I will find a station. Then you leave it alone. (*She leans over the walker precariously, adjusts the radio, then straightens herself up. She shuffles back to* PADRE *who has taken a seat on one end of the couch.*) I will not be frightened by you.

PADRE: Good.
BONNIE: And you will leave first thing in the morning.

PADRE: Sure.

BONNIE: And when you're through eating, I want you to go to your room.

PADRE: You order your sister around, too?

CLOVER: (*Messes with the radio dial again, turns up the volume to static.*) Electric Hitler. Radio Hitler.

PADRE: (*Watches* BONNIE *cross to the radio and repeat her adjustment of it.*) Got a net over your sister's bed, huh?

BONNIE: (*Stops, looks back at* PADRE.) To save her life. How's that? Here: she's simple. I'm cripped. If Clover walks off at night, she'll fall into a well pit or, if she wanders just afar as the mine shaft, then she's gone.

CLOVER: (*Sings.*) I walkin' the floor over you...

BONNIE: (*Adjusts the radio.*) Clover, leave it alone this time!

15

CLOVER: Electric stop. By Hitler.

BONNIE: Clover, that's not true. That's just something Berry said about the static. It's not true.

CLOVER: Berry lie?

BONNIE: No, Berry did not lie. It was a joke. Funny story.

CLOVER: Berry say Clover go far off and Hitler get Clover.

BONNIE: Yes, you stay inside unless I go outside.

CLOVER: No, Bonnie. Hitler sopped down radio.

BONNIE: Listen to the radio, Clover. But do not mess with it at all. Or it's time for bed.

PADRE: (*As* BONNIE *shuffles back toward the couch.*) Where was you two born?

BONNIE: (*Sitting on the opposite end of the couch.*) What difference that make?

PADRE: I got a do-it-yourself kind a cure.

BONNIE: For those who won't let you touch them?

PADRE: You take one disfigured or one fevered or one broken in any way, and you take that person or that child, take her back to where she was born. You roll that girl on the ground, roll her once toward each of the four directions. You do it in a holy way.

BONNIE: That's in the Bible?

(CLOVER, *fed up with the radio and the dials, walks out toward the unseen stairs, without being noticed by* BONNIE.)

PADRE: No, it's not.

BONNIE: Just something you made up.

PADRE: I get visions.

BONNIE: And then you get to try them out, right? It gives you influence over them, right?

PADRE: That cure is from a vision.

BONNIE: Finish eating.

PADRE: I learned 'bout visions from Indians… up in South Dakota. And from the Apache. And from the Cree in Canada.

BONNIE: Are you perfect?

17

PADRE: Nope. One time I said I'd shoot this guy in the
left ear from across a barroom. But I missed. I shot his
right ear.

BONNIE: Thank you for the introduction to your true self.
PADRE: You know where your true heart is?

BONNIE: It's late.

PADRE: Touch your heart.

BONNIE: What?

PADRE: Grab here. (*He grips his left upper chest.*)

BONNIE: I'm not going to grab myself there. And I won't
touch you.

PADRE: Don't you ever touch your chest to feel your
heartbeat?

BONNIE: I wouldn't do it with you here.

PADRE: Ever touch your left breast when you're alone?

BONNIE: Not for lack of someone else.

PADRE: Almost two years ago to the day -Pearl Harbor
sure changed things- I married Gene Tierney to Oleg Cassini.

Down in Vegas. I had this feeling something was wrong, but I couldn't quite reckon it out. So I had Gene touch Oleg's left chest and he had to put his palm on her breast. This was before the ceremony of marriage.

BONNIE: You married Gene Tierney, the movie star? (*Pause.*) No, you didn't.

PADRE: And the next day, baseball's Lou Gehrig died. That was what was causing that feeling I had about something being off. Now then, if I was to put my hand on your breast right now…

BONNIE: Don't!

PADRE: It won't hurt.

BONNIE: Please, I'm cripped-up.

PADRE: If you'll allow me, I'll know what's wrong.

BONNIE: No… you can't help.

(CLOVER *enters, holding* PADRE'S *canvas-over-burlap sack.* BONNIE *and* PADRE *are gazing into each other's eyes as his hand extends toward her breast.*)

CLOVER: Split head!

BONNIE: Put down his sack, Clover!

PADRE: And the child saw the face of evil.

CLOVER: Ring, ring, ring,
           The Farmer all dead.

(CLOVER *opens the sack and dumps out a decapitated head. The head is mottled, yellowish-green with purple spots.* BONNIE *screams and screams.* CLOVER *kneels beside the head as* PADRE *goes to it and puts it back into the sack.*)

CLOVER: Hitler-head, Hitler-head, Hitler-head,
           I walkin' the floor over you.

(PADRE, *with the head now sacked, returns to the screaming* BONNIE, *and he clamps a hand over her mouth and she tries to push him away.* CLOVER *places her hands over her ears.*)

PADRE: He was a draft dodger! Listen! It's my job. I go after draft dodgers. For our gover'ment. For Roosevelt. (*Pause.*) I'm going to take my hand away. I want you to stop screaming.

(PADRE *takes his hand away.* BONNIE *stares at the sack.*)

PADRE: What I do is legal… part of law.

(PADRE *takes a badge from his pocket and shows it to* BONNIE, *but she shows no recognition of having perceived it.*)

PADRE: I'm what you call an ad hoc federal officer. I hate this, too. But it must be done. For our Draft Boards. When draft dodgers won't come with me, when a man tries to take me on…. Please, try to understand. I'm a man of God. A padre.

CLOVER: Padre.

PADRE: Listen to your sister, Bonnie. These are days of daring. Be brave. Dare.

CLOVER: Padre.

(PADRE *turns the radio on to a slow waltz. He takes* CLOVER'S *hand.*)

PADRE: Let's dance.

(PADRE *and* CLOVER *dance for a beat, with halting formality.* BONNIE *comes to her senses, rises with great effort off the couch, forgets about the walker and lurches toward them, taking two or three steps before falling.*)

BONNIE: Noooo!

(BONNIE *weeps.* PADRE *lifts her to her feet, holds her up.*)

21

PADRE: As it says in the Bible, "And the king was pretty much moved, so he walked up to the bedroom over the gate, and the king cried. And he said to this young, crippled woman, he says, 'O young woman, if it's God's will, I'd die for you, you who are fair in His eyes.'"

BONNIE: (*Softly moans.*) Noooo.

PADRE: And now fair woman, walk for me. Walk for your sister. (*He steps back, prepared to catch her.*) Walk, I say!

BONNIE: (*Takes a step, wobbles, takes another step.*) Monster… bloody monster.

(BONNIE *takes another step as* PADRE *backs away from her.* CLOVER *goes to the radio, which has lost its volume, and she turns up the music, but static returns.*)

CLOVER: Electric fuzz. Hitler head!

(CLOVER *slaps the radio and music returns.* PADRE *moves in and catches BONNIE as she starts to collapse on yet another step, as she tried to punch at him. The lights flicker. The sound of thunder.* PADRE *waltzes BONNIE.*)

BONNIE: Dream…

PADRE: You're dancing. Your legs are working. Give thanks.

(PADRE *waltzes* BONNIE *to the bed.* CLOVER *pulls the rope and the net canopy falls over them. Then there is lightening and a horrendous thunderclap. The lights go out.*)

CLOVER: Help! Bonnie! Electric all gone.

(*The lights come back on.* BONNIE *is on top of* PADRE. *They stare into each other's eyes.*)

PADRE: "Then I spake to her of captivity and of all the things the Lord had showed me." Ezekiel. (*He strokes* BONNIE'S *hair.*) Give thanks, Bonnie. Let us both pray.

(*With* CLOVER *coming to the net and then holding onto it,* BONNIE *and* PADRE *enter a prolonged kiss.*)

CLOVER: Love me, O love me sad.
　　　　　Love me all heart.
　　　　　Love me all heart
　　　　　'cause I don' like sad.

(*Suddenly* BERRY *barges in through the door, dressed in well-worn cattleman's clothes and a cowboy hat. He has a rifle. He charges the net cage.* CLOVER *is surprised… stands aside.* PADRE *tries to get out from under* BONNIE, *but she has a tight grip on him.*)

CLOVER: Berry! Bonnie walk. Bonnie and love.

BERRY: Son of a bitch, you killed one of my men!

(*With* BERRY'S *rifle trained on him,* PADRE *finally disentangles himself.*)

PADRE: Put it up. I'm gover'ment law. He was wanted.

BERRY: Stand away from her. You fuckin' took that boy's head… sawed it off… maybe before he was even dead.

CLOVER: Berry drive Hudson. Clover like dance. Happy dance.

(CLOVER *attaches herself to* BERRY.)

BONNIE: Berry, I can walk!

PADRE: Take the boy's head. In the sack, buckaroo. Take it. As a present.

(BERRY *backs toward the sack, keeps his rifle trained on* PADRE. CLOVER *holds onto* BERRY'S *shirt.*)

CLOVER: Ghost town. Sing. Dance. Bonnie dance. Kiss.

BONNIE: (*Manages to get off the bed, stand, and takes a clumsy step.*)

BERRY: (*To* PADRE.) You're goin' to Hell.

PADRE: Naw. I pray to St. Joseph. He's got leverage… a daddy or sorts. Mary has to do what Joseph asks. Jesus has to be a loyal son. It's all worked-out: God has to let into Heaven anybody who prays to Joseph. (*In slow motion,* PADRE *goes for his belly gun.*) Look at the wanted posters on the desk. You were harboring a draft dodger.)

(PADRE, *in slow motion, brings his pistol to bear on* BERRY.)

BONNIE: Noooo!

LIGHTS SNAP TO BLACK: <u>THE END</u>

The Only Waco Delaney

Time: 1948

Locale: Gleeson, Arizona

Characters: WACO DELANEY, 72, a miner
NOTCH LANE, 35, Cochise County Sheriff
HELEN MARSHALL, 30, recruiter for the
Arizona Pioneers' Home in Prescott

The Only Waco Delaney was first produced by State University
of New York at Fredonia on March 6, 1995. The producing
director was Thomas W. Loughlin. The play was directed by
Jeff McConnell with the following cast:

Waco Delaney	Thomas W. Loughlin
Notch Lane	Jason Ostrowski
Helen Marshall	Melissa K. Miller

(*Upstage is a projection of a 1948 Arizona license plate. In filthy, stained miner's clothes, hair self-cropped and unwashed,* WACO *settles into a rickety old wooden gambling hall type wooden chair. He has an old, black iron fry pan filled with lard-fried hog ears. He has an old whiskey jug at his side.* WACO *begins to suck on the hog ear he takes from the fry pan. After a beat, he notices someone in the distance. He checks a nearby table, then looks at a pickax on the ground on his other side. He rises, gets a small sawed-off Colt from the table, sits again, and places the revolver under a leg. He resumes eating.* NOTCH LANE *and* HELEN MARSHALL *enter.* NOTCH *is wearing a lawman's uniform and badge with a holstered pistol, and he also has on boots and a Stetson hat.* HELEN *is wearing a 1940's Western-style sunsuit.* NOTCH *and* HELEN *are windblown… hot and tired from a long drive and from walking at least 200 yards in 100-degree heat.*)

NOTCH: Hello, Waco.

WACO: Baloney!

NOTCH: I brought a lady who wants to meet you.

WACO: (*Looks at* HELEN.) What you want?

HELEN: My name is Helen. I've heard so much about you.

WACO: Notch, I'm havin' supper. (*To* HELEN) Not enough to share. Sorry. (*To* NOTCH) Best to never forget supper. Visitors? Don't need any.

NOTCH: We come a long, hot way. We won't be long.

WACO: Hope so.

NOTCH: Helen Marshall, I want you to meet the last great prospector in Cochise County. This here is the legend. This here is The Only Waco Delaney. The last man in the field here at Gleeson. A true pioneer and…

WACO: It's mostly true. So what?

HELEN: I was driving through. Sheriff Lane said that I should meet you.

WACO: Could a waited for him to arrest me. He does that. Once a year. Twice a year. Sometimes more.

NOTCH: Now, Waco, I have never arrested you.

WACO: That's right. But you want to.

NOTCH: Miss Marshall, I near growed up in this town.

WACO: (*Points.*) Notch had the drizzlin' shits over there. Right in his gambler-stripe trousers. How old was you, Notch? Right there. His daddy 'n Notch, they come up here on a pair of crow-baits.

NOTCH: We're all young once. We all get old.

WACO: Now that we done history… 'n philosophy, tell the lady I got no lost gold mine tales to tell. None. The water table here is high and I got no deep shafts. Tell her. I can see she works for a livin'. I don't approve. When the communists take over, all the women'll work. Bet on it. This is a free country, so women who work must be communist. Lady, I want Notch to arrest you for bein' a communist. You understand that?

NOTCH: Waco, she ain't no communist.

WACO: She ain't?

HELEN: No.

WACO: I can tell from her outfit she ain't no cowgirl. And she don't remind me of Cattle Tooth Ruth over in Bisbee. You a bill collector for Cattle Tooth Ruth? That it? Now Notch, you may not believe it, but I ain't paid for a sweetheart since Tojo bombed us. Course I'd take love if it showed up here.

NOTCH: I doubt love comes to Gleeson anymore.

WACO: Ain't my fault. Don't you blame me. There was love here when I came in the spring of aught-one! Plenty of love… because we was all findin' gold. (*Pause.*) Say, Notch, you bring me a present?

NOTCH: (*Gets a sack of Mail Pouch chewing tobacco out of his back pants pocket.*) Sorry I sat on your chew.

WACO: So long's you didn't gas it.

NOTCH: (*Handing* WACO *the chewing tobacco.*) Helen is here on work. I'll admit it.

WACO: I got rights to all of Gleeson.

HELEN: I don't work in mining.

WACO: Attorney?

HELEN: No. I kind of bring happiness.

WACO: You bring happiness?

HELEN: Yes. As a messenger.

WACO: I hate happiness. Happiness is phony. Phony baloney! So sell me somethin' more pleasurin'.

NOTCH: Waco, I want you to hear Helen out.
WACO: Notch, if you wasn't raised near… in this town, I'd give you the boot. I might yet. You brought this woman to sell me somethin' I don't need. That ain't fair.

NOTCH: (*Pause.*) I can't look the other way anymore.

WACO: I get it. This is the roust.

HELEN: Sheriff, may I speak to Waco alone?

NOTCH: I do not advise that. And before this gets further, Waco, lemme have your ready.

WACO: My ready is in the provisions box.

(NOTCH *slowly gets in close and lifts* WACO'S *gun leg, and he takes the pistol.*)

NOTCH: No offense, Waco. It was making me nervous.

WACO: Lady, you did not bring happiness.

NOTCH: Goddamn, listen. This is hard for me. I'm tryin' to do somethin' that may be tough on you for a while, but you'll thank me.

HELEN: Waco, I represent the Arizona Pioneer's Home in Prescott. Have you heard of us?

NOTCH: She's got brochures in the patrol car.

WACO: Never heard a it.

HELEN: Sheriff Lane phoned us… about you. Bragged about all you've lived through. We'd like to invite you to live with us.

WACO: I got a choice?

NOTCH: Afraid not.

HELEN: Yes, you do.

WACO: No thanks.

NOTCH: Listen to her pitch.

WACO: My mind's set.

HELEN: You'll have your own room. It'll have a modern, comfortable bed, a lovely dresser, a nice closet, heat in the winter, a ceiling fan for summer, though Prescott doesn't heat up like down here. You'd receive a brand new radio, too!

WACO: I hate radio! I sing for myself!

HELEN: Two dollars a week spending money. Free chewing tobacco in our superintendant's office. The discipline is easy. No one tries to change you. This is a special place for very important pioneers… like you, Waco.

NOTCH: Waco, this is the best I could do.

WACO: The best? What in termite-fucks-burro are you tellin' me?

NOTCH: (*Pulls a hog ear from the fry pan.*) One complaint too many.

WACO: Send your complainer out here!

NOTCH: I told you it'd come to this.

WACO: My mess of hog ears is legal. Someone's settin' me up.

NOTCH: You got paperwork?

WACO: To hell with paperwork.

NOTCH: I got photographic evidence. Someone cut five ears off a Webb's hogs.

WACO: Think I could walk ten miles back after ten miles there, all for only five ears?

NOTCH: Yes, I do.

WACO: I can. But I didn't. A fellow came through, drivin' hogs at night to Tombstone. I gave gold dust for one hog, plus three ears.

NOTCH: Where's the hog?

WACO: It run off. Neglected to jab it. Tried takin' its ears first.

HELEN: Waco, the others at the Home, they're excited to meet you. Dogie Ed Lemmons, Six-Shooter Smith, Whisperin' Bill Stephens, and Gena Frazier. Gena still plays the piano! It's not really an old folks home. You'd never be lonely.

WACO: Lonesome don't matter.

NOTCH: (*Pulls paper from his shirt.*) This is a warrant for your arrest, Waco.

WACO: Can I have my ready back?

NOTCH: Two choices: jail or Prescott.

HELEN: Sheriff, I won't take him if he doesn't care to come.

WACO: Both a you, you're hereby evicted. Git!

(HELEN *begins to exit.*)

WACO: If your daddy was here, he'd help me!

NOTCH: Need help standing?

(WACO *stands on his own, slowly, and he looks around.*)

WACO: How much jail time?

NOTCH: Five months… maybe a year.

WACO: You know it can't be that a-way a-tall? (*Calls to* HELEN.) Say, Lady! Come on back.

NOTCH: If you go, Waco, I promise to visit regular. I'll bring top-shelf whiskey… and <u>fresh</u> chew.

(HELEN *returns.*)

HELEN: There's a saloon only half a mile from our front door.

WACO: I get time to pack?

NOTCH: Sure.

WACO: Can't leave my camp a mess.

HELEN: And this mining claim will be yours until you sell it or give it or leave it to someone. No one else can touch it.

NOTCH: I checked and Helen's right.

WACO: Maybe I can come back after this blows over.

NOTCH: He's The Only Waco Delaney, Miss Marshall!

WACO: If a jail sentence would be a year, then I ought to be able to come back in a year, right?

NOTCH: Waco fought off claim-jumpers and Apaches.

WACO: Notch, don't make this worse. Apaches were largely gone when I come here. (*Pause.*) I was the wildest thing here.

HELEN: Would you like some help packing?

WACO: Sure. Go on over to that general store. I bunk there. Be right behind you.

(HELEN *exits. The men watch her.*)

NOTCH: Good decision.

WACO: Sturdy woman.

NOTCH: Yes.

WACO: Ain't had one since Pearl Harbor Day. Haven't had one that sturdy… not with all her teeth… not since Hoover. And you?

NOTCH: We better help her pack your stuff.

WACO: Can you see me there, see me playin' with my fingernails? Droolin' on my shirt? (*Pause.*) I was about to get me a dog.

(WACO, *slowly at first, picks up the pickax. He starts to take a swing at* NOTCH, *who easily grabs it. There is a brief struggle.* WACO *loses his grip on the pickax, sits on the ground, claws his chest, breathes hard.* HELEN *comes running.*)

HELEN: Oh, no. He's having a heart attack.

(NOTCH *gently lifts* WACO.)

WACO: Lemme die here. Hosses are all a-stampedin'.

(NOTCH *and* HELEN, *almost tenderly, hold* WACO *from each side.*)

WACO: Scare-up a hoss for me to die on.

HELEN: Will he make it?

NOTCH: Waco, cut this out.

WACO: Lemme walk. (*Steady on his feet now, he takes a step from them.*) Go 'head, use the damn-it-to-hell cuffs. I want the dignity of my capture.

HELEN: No! He can't travel in handcuffs!

WACO: Okay… I'm gonna escape.

(WACO *takes off in a tottering run, but is easily caught by* NOTCH.)

NOTCH: Here's a deal: you can have the hog ears to eat. But don't make me use the cuffs.

WACO: Fuck the hog ears. You cuff me. Someone's got to remember. This way you'll remember. You'll remember you pissed on me. You piss on The Only Waco Delaney, you piss on all a Arizona Territory! You can tell your kids a version of the truth. You can brag. You can say, "I caught 'n cuffed The Only Waco Delaney, outlaw-prospector." (*He takes a futile swing at* NOTCH,)

HELEN: Don't hit him back!

(NOTCH *handcuffs* WACO, *in front, and* WACO *slowly raises his hands toward the sky, as if for a blessing.*)

LIGHTS SNAP TO BLACK: <u>THE END</u>

Rooster and Ponytail

Time: 1958

Locale: Mullen, Nebraska

Characters: PONYTAIL, 15, a schoolgirl
             ROOSTER, 21, a killer
             FR. SNOW, 79, a Catholic priest

Rooster and Ponytail was first produced by the University of
Nevada, Las Vegas, on May 9, 1991. It was directed by
Davey Marlin-Jones with the following cast:

Ponytail	Kymm Gant
Rooster	Todd Espeland
Fr. Snow	Evan McDonnell

(Upstage is a massive painting of a blood-splattered 1958 Nebraska license plate, which bears the slogan, "The Beef State." The plate, black numbers on white, has a bullet hole. As lights rise we see a roadside café in or near Mullen, Nebraska: a lunch counter with a covered pie and a pot of coffee, and there are a couple of enamel-white café tables with enamel-white chairs. As lights rise, the owner-cook is crumpled on the floor over a pool of blood, quite dead. Facing downstage, a Classic Comic Book in one hand, PONYTAIL stares at the body. She is wholesome, dressed in jeans, plaid shirt, an unzipped winter jacket, and sneakers that have a couple of holes.)

PONYTAIL: *(Calls out.)* Rooster? *(Listens. No response.)* We gonna be here long?

(ROOSTER appears from behind the license plate. He is 5'5" at most in bare feet, but he's a few inches taller, thanks to very over-size cowboy boots stuffed with newspapers. ROOSTER is also wearing jeans, a stained cream-colored pullover sweater, and an unzipped black leather jacket. His hair is short on top and long on the sides, combed and slicked back into a duck tail. In one hand he has a .22 revolver and he has a sawed-off .410 in his other hand.)

ROOSTER: Find any Winstons? *(She shakes her head.)* I thought you was gonna look. *(Pause.)* Whatch ya been doin'?

PONYTAIL: I think I'm sick.

ROOSTER: On-the-rag? (*Pause.*) If so, we can stop somewhere for that stuff. (*No response from her.*) <u>Hey!</u> What is it?

PONYTAIL: Nothing.

ROOSTER: (*Sets his .22 down on the counter, rummages.*) Damn. (*Shrugs. Finds a newspaper, pulls it up.*) Hope it's today's paper. Yep. <u>Look!</u> They got pictures of us on page one! Ain't that something? (*Pause.*) Ya wanna know what they say? (*Pause.*) Hey, don't look at him. He ain't movin'. Come here. Read me what it says. (*Pause.*) <u>Come here!</u>

(PONYTAIL *walks to* ROOSTER *and he hands the paper to her.*)

PONYTAIL: (*She looks at the paper .*) It says we killed six. (*She stares at the body.*)

ROOSTER: They given us some extras there. We only done three.

PONYTAIL: (*Again looking at the newspaper.*) They're counting the kid at the gas station, and…

ROOSTER: The gas station was back in December. That ain't the same. It was weeks ago!

PONYTAIL: The two that was parked.

ROOSTER: They deserved it, what with them snotty and them havin' a new car and money. They never earned that stuff.

PONYTAIL: And that salesman, whose Ford we got.

ROOSTER: But we got different plates on 'er.

PONYTAIL: Yes.

ROOSTER: I count four on that. Who else we blamed for?

PONYTAIL: Rooster…. You promised…. You said, "I'll just take 'em to the garage 'n lock 'em up." You promised on your heart.

ROOSTER: That's what I done.

PONYTAIL: They say you shot Momma and Daddy.

ROOSTER: <u>They're lyin'</u>!

PONYTAIL: You <u>promised</u>! You said if I came with you they'd be cold, but okay.

ROOSTER: It's a trick!

PONYTAIL: … and my baby sister… (*Suddenly she sobs.*)

47

ROOSTER: (*Snatches the paper from her and tosses it away, individual pages fluttering over the body.*) <u>Lies</u>!

PONYTAIL: (*Through her sobs.*) … my baby sister was killed by a rifle butt smashing-in her head.

ROOSTER: No! You gotta believe me. I'd never do that!

PONYTAIL: But you and Momma were fighting.

ROOSTER: That's why I locked 'em up. That's what a sheriff does. He locks 'em up until they cool off. (*Pause.*) Can't ya see? They're tryin' to cut us in half. They want you to leave me. It's a trick. That's all it is. (*No response. Pause.*) Ponytail, pretty baby, I can prove it. When we get to Wyoming. We find a pay phone. You talk to them. They'll be mad. So you can't tell where we are, okay? But you can talk to 'em. And then I'll tell your old lady, "What the hell you up to with lies like this?" She should a never let the paper say she's killed. It's not right. (*He puts his arm around her.*) We blasted only four, countin' Mr. Café here, but they don't know that yet. So the real dead count is only three.

PONYTAIL: Rooster, please. Take me to a hospital. You don't have to come in. You can just drive off. I won't tell them who I am. I'll give them another name.

ROOSTER: I can't leave you.

PONYTAIL: Please.

ROOSTER: Just can't. You're the spark… the thrill. What's been missin' from me. You're only <u>feelin'</u> sick. (*He touches her forehead.*)

PONYTAIL: My stomach hurts.

ROOSTER: You don't have no fever. You're gonna be okay. Think about good things. Think about when we're gonna be out in Washington or Oregon. We'll call ourselves Mr. & Mrs. Smith… something like that. A real common name, but not Smith. Smith's not such a good one. But think about us sittin' by the ocean. Just us and the waves. We'll find us two snobby kids and kill 'em. And we'll put 'em in our car. They'll have our clothes and personal stuff. We'll set the car on fire 'n roll it over a cliff. We'll be completely new people. We'll have hold-up money. We'll buy us a house on the ocean, Ponytail. With loads a windows, a big TV and record player combo… and <u>all</u> the records Elvis ever sung. We can't ever go back. There ain't nothin' back there for us.

(PONYTAIL *rushes to the counter and vomits over the counter… behind it.* ROOSTER *comforts her. When she is done, he takes out a red bandana and wipes her brow and mouth. He kisses the soiled bandana and tosses it at the body.*)

ROOSTER: I love you.

PONYTAIL: Please, Rooster. I'll say it wasn't even you.

ROOSTER: But it was me. It was both of us. But it was me. That's okay. The people need to know it was me. They're gonna say we had no choices. Like in the Old West. It was those people or us. (*He goes behind the counter and rummages, then holds up a pair of scissors.*) Thought I spotted these. I got eagle eyes. (*He goes to the scattered newspaper sheets and finds page one. He takes it to her.*) Gimme your hand.

(PONYTAIL *gives her hand to* ROOSTER *and he places it on the scissors. He guides her as they cut out the pictures of themselves. He tosses the scissors over the counter.*)

PONYTAIL: They say you might've kidnapped me.

ROOSTER: Another of their lies.

PONYTAIL: Sure. And if you drop me off somewhere, I'll tell 'em it ain't true.

ROOSTER: (*With his free hand, he holds up the newspaper pictures.*) You been in the paper 'fore?

PONYTAIL: No.

ROOSTER: Then we need to trade pictures. You take mine and I'll keep your picture.

(ROOSTER *hands* PONYTAIL *his clipped picture. He then places her picture in one of his jacket pockets. She watches him and then folds his picture and puts it in one of her jacket pockets. They tenderly kiss.* ROOSTER *then sets the .410 on the counter and picks up the .22 pistol. He walks a few feet, turns towards the body.*)

ROOSTER: (*To the corpse.*) Hombre, you done crossed the wrong man. (*Pause.*) Draw! (*He quick-draws… as if from a holster.*) Bang! (*To* PONYTAIL.) No sense wastin' another round on him, is there? (*Pause.*) Just think: when we push that car off some cliff with those kids we'll catch, the law will think it's us. The newspapers will say it was like the way James Dean died. You like that?

PONYTAIL: (*Nods.*) You know how you always tell me you love me? How you'll do anything for me?

ROOSTER: That's exactly how we are.

PONYTAIL: Then take us out of here.

ROOSTER: Yeah, we're gonna go. But not 'till just 'fore dawn.

PONYTAIL: What about him?

ROOSTER: He won't start to stink for a while. (*Pause.*) This is our stop for the night. It got the "Closed" sign on the door. We got food. We can sleep. We'd freeze in the

51

car. We gotta stop here. We deserve it: all this warmth 'n
food. Come mornin' we'll drive out. Get some Winstons.

PONYTAIL: I'm scared.

ROOSTER: (*He sets the .22 pistol on the counter, gently goes to her.*)
Don't know why, but bein' with you is like ownin' a little
world all our own. Like when we're lyin' there with our arms
'round each other, not talkin' much, just kind a tightenin' up
'n listenin' to the wind blow. Like in that field of prairie
grass.

PONYTAIL: Bluestem.

ROOSTER: That's right: bluestem. Or when we're lookin'
at the same star. (*They kiss.*) I forget about my bowlegs
when we're havin' excitement.

(ROOSTER *slowly draws her parka off* PONYTAIL's *shoulders
and down her arms and it drops to the floor. He unbuttons her plaid
shirt and pulls it down her arms until it, too, drops to the floor, and he
kisses her shoulder.*

ROOSTER: When I hold you in my arms 'n we do the
things we done together, I never think how some people call
me "peckerwood." This world has given us to each other.

PONYTAIL: Yes, we give ourselves.

ROOSTER: We're gonna make this world leave us alone. If we'd been left alone in the first place, we wouldn't a hurt anybody.

(*They caress each other and turn so that* PONYTAIL *can see toward where the door is. Suddenly there is the sound of a ring being tapped on the glass, wood-framed door.* PONYTAIL *breaks the embrace.*)

PONYTAIL: Someone's here.

ROOSTER: Damn it, the sign says, "Closed."

(ROOSTER *tries to regain the embrace, but* PONYTAIL *steps back, covers her bra cups with her hands.*)

PONYTAIL: There's a man. He sees us.

ROOSTER: I better let him in.

PONYTAIL: No, Rooster. Let's run out the back. Let's get in the car and drive all night.

(*As* ROOSTER *walks to where the door is —offstage,* PONYTAIL *hurriedly puts her shirt back on,* ROOSTER *returns with* FR. SNOW, *who is dressed in a black, narrow-brim hat, black knee-length coat open at the front, black shirt with a Roman collar, black trousers and black shoes. The priest moves with stiffness earned with eighty years of living.* PONYTAIL, *as the men enter, picks up her coat and covers the guns.*)

ROOSTER: (*To* FR. SNOW.) You got my call then.

FR. SNOW: (*Suddenly seeing the body*). Call?

ROOSTER: Just called the church. Some guy said he'd find you.

FR. SNOW: A man was at the rectory?

ROOSTER: Well, yeah. You don't believe me? (*To* PONYTAIL.) We called for a priest, didn't we?

PONYTAIL: (*Briefly hesitates.*) Yes.

(FR. SNOW, *with difficulty from age, kneels by the body.*)

ROOSTER: It was an awful accident.

FR. SNOW: Poor, sweet Dexter.

ROOSTER: (*Also kneeling, on the other side of the body.*) He's my uncle. My own uncle Dexter. And he blowed himself up. I told him, "You don't want to hold that gun." I told him. So it's all my fault. See, I walked in here with a damned sawed-off .410. My girl 'n me, we spotted it roadside... on the road this side a Broken Bow.

FR. SNOW: All he wanted tonight was a game of poker.

ROOSTER: You gonna do that dead prayer or not?

FR. SNOW: He wasn't Catholic.

ROOSTER: Do it anyways. He wrote to me once, sayin' he was gonna turn Catholic. So how's that? (*To* PONYTAIL.) You know me. I'm real acceptin' of others and all.

FR. SNOW: Have you called the sheriff?

ROOSTER: Uh... no. We was waitin' for you. You need to tell the sheriff how it was. An accident. And she's my witness.

FR. SNOW: (*With effort he awkwardly stands.*) I'll fetch the sheriff.

ROOSTER: No! You go sit at that table! (*He half-shoves the priest to one of the tables.*)

FR. SNOW: Why? What was gained in the murder of this good man?

ROOSTER: <u>Listen</u> to me, old man, this ain't <u>murder</u>! (*He goes to the guns, flips the jacket off them, hands* PONYTAIL *the .410, then speaks to her.*) Keep this aimed at him. If he moves, blast him. (*Pause.*) We got some thinkin' to do. And I can't think on an empty stomach. (*He exits behind the huge license plate.*)

FR. SNOW: You're the two teenagers from Lincoln.

PONYTAIL: Please, don't talk.

FR. SNOW: Please... hand me the shotgun. Then go outside and run.

PONYTAIL: I don't want to kill you.

(PONYTAIL *raises the shotgun and sights* FR. SNOW *in. He closes his eyes. Pause. She lowers the shotgun and he opens his eyes.*).

FR. SNOW: Is he your first boyfriend? (*No response from her.*) Sometimes we need to talk most when we are most afraid to.

PONYTAIL: Had dates 'fore Rooster. (*Pause.*) I was going to break up with Rooster. That's what started it. Momma was tellin' Rooster to get out. They started yelling. And my daddy, he's really my stepdaddy, my real daddy's dead, he slaps Rooster. That's when Rooster goes to his car... brings in this gun.

FR. SNOW: My father died, too, when I was young. Drowned on a cattle drive. Crossing the Red River.

PONYTAIL: Did it change you? Make you do strange things? (*Pause*). I don't like it when people assume it does stuff to you. (*Pause.*) Is my Momma and Daddy dead?

FR. SNOW: Child, I'm very sorry.

PONYTAIL: No, no…. It can't be. It's just a lie the papers are tellin'.

(ROOSTER *returns, balancing three plates and forks. The plates are loaded with cold chicken, donuts, and chips. He sets a plate down on the counter for* PONYTAIL *and brings a plate to* FR. SNOW.)

ROOSTER: (*To* PONYTAIL.) You can go eat now. (*To* FR. SNOW.) I ain't that bad a guy. I ain't a threat to society. You got the wrong misunderstanding. (*He backs to the counter, sets his plate down, takes the .410, and places it on his lap… pointed at the priest.*) You think guys like me 'n James Dean get to Heaven?

FR. SNOW: I don't get to vote on that.

ROOSTER: (*Stands and points the shotgun at* FR. SNOW). I could kill you right now!

PONYTAIL: Rooster, No!

ROOSTER: But I won't… maybe. (*Pause.*) See, I'm a lot like Jesse James and them ol' time heroes. (*Pause.*) Want me to prove it?

FR. SNOW: No need to prove anything.

ROOSTER: That's right. Glad you know that. The Rooster don't have to do nothin'. But here's the deal: I <u>am</u> gonna prove it. Take out your wallet.

FR. SNOW: You'll be disappointed.

ROOSTER: Don't stall. I ain't some peckerwood! Gimme your goddamned wallet!

PONYTAIL: Please do it.

(FR. SNOW *takes out his wallet and places it on the edge of his table.* ROOSTER *motions* PONYTAIL *over to get it. She brings the wallet to* ROOSTER, *who looks inside it.*)

ROOSTER: What we got here is a Father Snow. (*He takes out the folding money… a ten, a five, and two ones. He pauses to look at the priest.*) When's your next payday?

FR. SNOW: Next week.

ROOSTER: You got more cash at home? (*Then to* PONYTAIL.) Eat some a that.

FR. SNOW: Ten or so dollars.

ROOSTER: If I was to give all this back to you, would ya give some a it to charity… say ten?

FR. SNOW: If you wish me to.

ROOSTER: Here's the nutshell: my pretty baby 'n me, we need gas money for the mornin'. By me taking some a your money, I won't need to hold-up anybody. So I'm gonna take five-dollars. (*He stuffs the five-dollar bill into one of his pockets.*) And I'm givin' the rest back, but you gotta give five of it to charity, okay?

FR. SNOW: Yes.

ROOSTER: (*To* PONYTAIL.) See, it's like I told you I am.

(ROOSTER *gathers the money he's set on the counter, puts it back into the wallet, and underhands it onto the priest's table. He goes behind the counter and gets three bottles of Pepsi, opens them, and hands them out.*)

FR. SNOW: I can leave now?

ROOSTER: If I was cruel, like the way police are, I'd show you a mean trick, Father Snow. They pick up a guy, 'n you know how they get a confession? They tilt the guy back in a chair. Then they pour the sodie pop down his nose while they gag his mouth. It feels like your head's explodin' is what it feels like!

PONYTAIL: Please, Rooster, let him be.

ROOSTER: (*To* PONYTAIL.) I was just explainin'. (*To* FR. SNOW.) Go 'head, eat. (*No response from the priest.*) <u>Eat</u>!

FR. SNOW: Please, leave here without the guns. Leave right now. I won't get the sheriff until morning. Leave without the guns. Leave the girl with me. Just go off and…

ROOSTER: And enjoy this world? You still don't understand. Except for Ponytail here, I don't believe I ever would a found a good personal world. (*Pause.*) We don't really know life… or what life is to us. People like you keep preachin' this is a wonderful world to live in, but I don't believe I ever did really live in a wonderful world.

FR. SNOW: Did murdering Dexter make it better?

ROOSTER: Oh, hell, this café cook just happened to be here. <u>I</u> didn't put him here. Maybe you say God did. But I didn't ask him to be here when he should a been home, and he didn't know me 'n Ponytail was comin'.

FR. SNOW: Give up your hatred, Rooster. Give up your guns.

ROOSTER: I have hated 'n been hated. And now I gotta keep alive my little world as long as possible. I got my guns. That's my answer. The more I look at people, the more I hate 'em in return. I always knowed they ain't a place for me, but there is a person for me: Ponytail. But the other people… I used to wonder why they was here anyhow. Bunch of goddamned fools, always makin' fun a some poor guy who ain't done nothin' but feed chickens 'n hogs. (*Long pause.*) And tonight, Father Snow, you're gonna marry us!

FR. SNOW: It won't be valid.

ROOSTER: (*To* PONYTAIL.) The rest a the way, it'll be our honeymoon. (*To* FR. SNOW) I'm gonna show you real love. (*To* PONYTAIL.) Come to me, dream girl. (*She slowly goes to him.*) Go 'head, baby. Do what ya do.

PONYTAIL: Let's tie up the priest, Rooster. Then we drive off 'n I'll do it.

ROOSTER: Here!

PONYTAIL: Not here.

FR. SNOW: Please, shoot me first.

ROOSTER: This ain't a dyin' thing, priest. Baby, you ashamed?

PONYTAIL: (*She takes a hair from one side of* ROOSTER'S *head and yanks it out. She holds it up as if to some god.*) I love this one hair. I love it even though it's the smallest part of Rooster. I love it like a weeping willow loves to reach down to earth. I love it like… (*She hesitates*).

61

ROOSTER: Say it!

PONYTAIL: …like I love to see you all naked, us naked in the hallway mirror when nobody's home. I love this hair like the whole life we're gonna live.

ROOSTER: (*To* FR. SNOW.) Now turn 'round 'n eat! You stop eating… and I kill you. That's what priests do: eat 'n drink too much. <u>Turn 'round</u>.! (*After the priest turns and faces downstage.*) Pretty baby, when our world ends, I want to go down shooting. With you there. I want to go down like that. For you.

(ROOSTER *leans over the counter and pulls up a radio. He turns it on and we hear a song from the country-pop charts of 1957-1958. The guns are on the counter.* ROOSTER *takes* PONYTAIL'S *hand, kisses it, and they slow dance. They begin to grind against each other. He takes her plaid shirt off and she unbuttons his jeans. They dance. They kiss. As the music fades, they move to the counter. She takes off his sweater and he is bare-chested. Meanwhile,* FR. SNOW *is head-down at the table, his hands covering his ears.* ROOSTER *moves the radio and the guns aside and helps* PONYTAIL *up onto the counter. They kiss. He pulls off her sneakers. He unbuttons her jeans, but she catches his hand near her crotch.*)

PONYTAIL: No, Rooster, not all the way… not all the way. (*She pushes at him.*)

ROOSTER: I feel it. Tonight's the night. We gotta.

PONYTAIL: No, please. Just kiss me.

(ROOSTER'S *mouth covers her mouth. While* ROOSTER *and* PONYTAIL *are making out,* FR. SNOW *stands and turns, picks up a chair and rushes toward* ROOSTER. ROOSTER *hears his approach and spins, catches the blow from the chair with his hands, wrests the chair away… and hurls it a few feet.)*

ROOSTER: And I trusted you!

(FR. SNOW *looks at* PONYTAIL, *who lowers her head, and he shuffles back to his table and sits.* PONYTAIL *gets off the counter, stands, arms limp at her sides.* ROOSTER *picks up the guns, takes the pistol to* FR. SNOW, *and sets it on the table in front of him.* PONYTAIL *sags to the floor, rolls into a fetal position.)*

ROOSTER: Father Snow, this is it. Now we get real Western. You go for the pistol when you see me raise up the .410. I'll keep it by my leg until you go for the pistol.

FR. SNOW: I beg you.

ROOSTER: You got to the count of five to draw, then I blow you all over this café. (*Pause.*) One…. Two…. Three…. Four….

(FR. SNOW *picks up the revolver and points it at* ROOSTER, *who laughs and keeps his shotgun barrel-down.)*

ROOSTER: Funny, ain't it? I can stand here all day 'n you won't shoot. (*Pause as they eyeball each other.*) Ponytail, looks like it's gonna work out. Get back up on that counter. Drink some sodie pop. Then we can share some personal excitement.

FR. SNOW: One last time, put the gun down.

ROOSTER: Hey, priest, your spine just got shit out your ass. (*To* PONYTAIL, *who does not move.*) We'll drive to the ocean, pretty baby. We'll walk where the waves hit the sand. (*Pause.*) Ponytail, I love you. I think we should have kids.

(PONYTAIL *remains in a fetal position. After a beat, she stands. She kisses* ROOSTER'S *cheek, takes his hand, then releases it. Buttoning her jeans, she walks downstage.*)

PONYTAIL: Sun's coming up, Rooster. Time for you to crow. Time for us to go.

(PONYTAIL *goes to* ROOSTER *and takes his shotgun. They get their clothes together... and all the while* FR. SNOW *has the revolver aimed at* ROOSTER. PONYTAIL, *one hand clasped to* ROOSTER'S *hand, leads him to the door. Suddenly* FR. SNOW *shoots* ROOSTER *in the back.* ROOSTER *turns, a hand outstretched to the priest.* PONYTAIL *sets down the .410 and goes to the now-face-down* ROOSTER, *and she slowly lies down beside him, one arm over a small pool of blood.*)

PONYTAIL: <u>Momma</u>!

LIGHTS SNAP TO BLACK: <u>THE END</u>

More Honky Tonk Scars

Time: 1981

Locale: Van Horn, Texas

Characters: NEWT, 23
　　　　　　　BECKY, 23
　　　　　　　HUB, 42, Becky's father
　　　　　　　PENNY, 18, Newt's wife

More Honky Tonk Scars was first produced by State University of New York at Fredonia on March 6, 1995. The producing director was Thomas W. Loughlin. The play was directed by Michele A. Helberg with the following cast:

Newt	Matthew C. Ralyea
Beckey	Stephanie I. Ludes
Hub	Evan K. Harrington
Penny	Amy Livingston

(Upstage is a slide projection of a 1981 Texas license plate. The projection is soon replaced with one of the back side of a honky-tonk. NEWT is tied to a lawn chair, a beer having recently been poured over his head; the longneck bottle is on his lap. Another five beers are beside him. Several other lawn chairs are nearby. He is wearing jeans, a snap shirt, boots, and his straw cowboy hat is stomped and nearby. BECKY enters, wearing a simple, low-cut, white summer dress.)

BECKY: *(Circles him.)* Near closin' time.

NEWT: That right?

BECKY: Yer rope?

NEWT: Yeah.

BECKY: Uh huh. *(She starts to untie him.)*

NEWT: Don't.

BECKY: *(Stops untying him.)* Big strappin' hoss like you, this don't seem right. *(Pause.)* Where's Penny? *(No response.)* Uh huh.

(HUB enters, wearing a hillbilly tuxedo jacket, jeans, boots. He looks at BECKY, then at NEWT, then he gets one of the lawn chairs and sits.)

NEWT: God a'mighty, have one of my beers.

69

HUB: (*Picks up a bottle, finds an opener, opens the beer, takes a drink.*) You got better 'n scant reason for this?

BECKY: Dad, want me to lock up?

HUB: Naw, Becky, sit on down.

BECKY: He don't want to be untied.

HUB: That so?

BECKY: Uh huh.

HUB: Boy, you're reekin' of beer.

BECKY: At least the neon ought to be shut off.

(HUB *motions to a lawn chair.*)

NEWT: I'm gonna kill him.

HUB: They in your Lincoln? Off to see the Marfa lights?

BECKY: (*Points.*) There's the Lincoln.

NEWT: She's got that gaudy dress on.

HUB: I noticed.

BECKY: Dad, you want a grilled steak or somethin'?

HUB: Well… I don't hear nothin'.

NEWT: Car windows is shut. Muffles the sound.

HUB: There's a kindness.

NEWT: Lyndon Rogers I'm gonna hang from a cottonwood. With this here rope.

HUB: He the one in there with her now?

BECKY: Dad, maybe we ought to call the law.

HUB: Newt, can Becky have one a your beers?

NEWT: Excuse my manners. Sure, Becky. Have one. (*He watches* HUB *open a beer and hand it to* BECKY.) And Ricky Endock I'm gonna burn over a mesquite fire.

BECKY: Ricky in the Lincoln with 'em, too?

NEWT: Naw. Penny says when she's finished doing Lyndon, she's gonna do Ricky. (*Pause.*) Then she says she'll be sending for Dale Haynes. Then Bud Walden. Dale I'm gonna skin, then tan his sorry ass.

HUB: 'n how you gonna kill Bud?

NEWT: Bud? Shit. I ain't gonna kill Bud. No.

HUB: Sure? Bud's as sorry as the other three.

NEWT: Sure is.

HUB: I get it. He's the only one a them's married. You're gonna fuck his Elma.

NEWT: I wouldn't fuck Elma Turnbow when we was in high school. Why'd I wanna fuck her now, Hub?

BECKY: Revenge.

NEWT: Naw, Bud'll have to go home to Elma. That's punishment 'nuff. She's big as two welded-together pick-up trucks. Elma's been on full feed her whole life. (*Pause.*) But Lyndon Rogers... he's the first. Lyndon's grazing on my woman right now, so he's the first. (*Pause.*) Y'all know what today is?

HUB: Newt, marriage is somethin' a man is supposed to endure. You 'n me both know you left here some nights with other 'n Penny. Guess I'm lucky you ain't left here with Becky. Course I'd a killed you.

NEWT: I've appreciated that.

BECKY: I'm the only woman in Van Horn who can't get lucky in this here honky-tonk.

HUB: Becky, get us some chili. Newt, you want a bowl, too?

BECKY: I ain't gettin' no chili.

HUB: (*Looks at her for a beat, then shrugs.*) Newt, how long we gotta wait? I mean, we can wait inside.

NEWT: It's a nice night out here.

BECKY: Why'd you marry Penny?

NEWT: Dunno. Tracie Flores… she moved to Alpine. Left me dumbstruck. Works a dude ranch. Takes tourists out on rattler hunts.

BECKY: You once promised to marry me, Newt.

HUB: What?!?!

NEWT: Ain't true.

BECKY: I wrote it down. Day 'n time. I wondered at it. What it'd be like to be Becky Rose 'stead of Becky Gomez.

HUB: When this go on?

BECKY: Fifth grade.

NEWT: You give me the nod?

BECKY: You seemed pretty hard-luck.

NEWT: Hub, they been at it some ten or so minutes. You wanna tell 'em to hurry up?

BECKY: You come outta that chute at the junior rodeo. Then the next thing: that steer is puttin' hooves to your face.

HUB: Chili'll require reheatin', Becky.

BECKY: Why don't you just get a divorce?

NEWT: No such thing. Married once, married always.

HUB: Not these days. Pope gives eliminations. You got to write to Rome, but I hear they's big-hearted these days. Hell, you and Penny ain't even got children yet. (*Pause.*) Unless one of them fellows workin' out in the Lincoln get you some in nine months.

NEWT: See, you don't know what today is.

HUB: Okay, you know what day today is. Fine. You got a wife wide-open, legs-spread, in your own goddamned car, but you know what today is.

BECKY: Don't be mean, Daddy. Maybe today is San Jacinto Day or somethin'.

HUB: It ain't no San Jacinto Day.

NEWT: It sure ain't. Today is my twenty-third goddamned, sorry birthday.

BECKY: Happy Birthday.

NEWT: That's what Penny says to me. She says, "Happy Birthday, Newt." Then she says she's got a surprise for me. But she's gotta tie me up, 'cause she knows it's gonna get me too excited.

(HUB *stands, exits.*)

BECKY: She must think you deserve this. (*Pause.*) She caught you, didn't she?

NEWT: It is foregone: a man is gonna be restless.

BECKY: You mean greedy. (*Pause.*) The only time you and I ever danced was at Homecoming.

NEWT: Your daddy is over to my Lincoln.

BECKY: I think you liked me better 'n Tracie Flores at Homecoming.

75

NEWT: Penny said she's gonna come back 'n untie me when she's done with fuckery. Says that'll be her final satisfaction of the night. Know what I'm gonna do? Nothin'. I ain't gonna do nothin' tonight.

BECKY: Good.

NEWT: But tomorrow.... Tomorrow, when she fries the same goddamned hotcakes that she cooks ever' mornin', I am gonna choke her on 'em. Yeah... I am going to choke her. First I am gonna rope her... and tie her to a kitchen chair. And then I am gonna mount her as she dies.

BECKY: I don't reckon you'll do any a that.

NEWT: You want a ticket? It'll be a tough way for her to expire.

(BECKY *stands... kisses* NEWT *long and hard, then sits down again.*)

BECKY: Not an entirely bad kiss, stupid.

NEWT: If Hub seen that, he'll knife his way through my belly.

BECKY: I just improved your birthday.

(HUB *returns.*)

HUB: Couldn't see a thing. Pretty steamy inside a your car. (*Picks up another beer and opens it.*) I did catch a word or two. (*Pause.*) Your wife's mad… 'cause her panties is tore.

NEWT: Torn panties? Lyndon Rogers ain't gonna live to see sunrise.

BECKY: Daddy, Newt kissed me while you was peepin' into the car.

HUB: Newt… he don't have the nerve. (*Looks at* NEWT.) Son, I got more honky-tonk scars than you can imagine.

NEWT: Yes, sir.

BECKY: I did kiss him, daddy. I was clingin' all over Newt… 'n my tongue tangled with his tongue.

(HUB *stands.*)

NEWT: Now, Hub, Becky's just jokin'.

(HUB *kicks* NEWT *and the chair over.*)

BECKY: Kick Newt 'nother time, I'm leavin'. You glare at ever' boy who even treats me to a smile. To hell with that!

HUB: Make better choices, Becky.

(The sound of a car door opening, then, after a beat, slamming shut.)

BECKY: Daddy, you gotta lift Newt back to where he was.

NEWT: My vision's blurred. Think you got my eye, Hub. But… but I been hurt much worse by bulls.

HUB: See, Becky, this boy likes pain. You went 'n kissed a pain-lover. Beats all.

(PENNY enters, sweaty, and her cheap sundress is wrinkled and off-kilter. PENNY is holding a revolver in one hand and a knife in her other hand.)

PENNY: Who gave you permission to move?

HUB: I kicked him over, Penny. He needed it… kissin' my Becky.

NEWT: You gonna untie me or not?

PENNY: I'm gonna <u>cut</u> you loose.

NEWT: Don't do that! I give over thirty-dollars for this lariat!

PENNY: You're gonna get into the car. Passenger side. I'm drivin'.

BECKY: Newt ain't goin' with you.

PENNY: (*Pause. Looks at* PENNY.) Jam a taco in your mouth 'fore my barker makes a bang.

HUB: Penny, how much you want to sell Newt for. I'll give, oh, twenty.

NEWT: Penny. Where is Lyndon off to?

BECKY: It's the principle. Newt figures he needs to kill Lyndon. But he don't. We can talk him out of that notion. See, Penny, I'm the girl Newt's really always wanted. But he's been too scared of Daddy. Penny, this is a good way out for you.

PENNY: A way out a this? What the fuck you fat-mouthin' 'bout? You just let me lesson my Newt.

(PENNY *leans down with the knife to cut the rope.* HUB *kicks her in the ribs, sends her sprawling. As* HUB *pulls* NEWT *up into normal sitting position,* PENNY *sits up, points the gun at them.*)

BECKY (*Pointing.*) There's the sheriff!

(*When* PENNY *turns to look,* BECKY *goes at her. The women spin.* HUB *wrests the gun away. The women separate. The knife is on the ground near* NEWT.)

NEWT: Untie me. I need to slap her for messin' up my new Bailey hat.

HUB: Newt, you're stayin' right in that chair. All night. (*To* PENNY.) I'm drivin' you home.

PENNY: Sounds real romantic. (*She exits.*)

HUB: Becky, leave him be. (*He exits.*)

NEWT: Your daddy gonna fuck my wife, too?

BECKY: Daddy ain't that sorry a man. But it gives you 'n me maybe twenty minutes. Then I'll tie you up again. (*Pause.*) You need a good luck angel. (*She gives him a long kiss.*)

NEWT: Okay... I'll pretend that you're Tracie Flores.

(BECKY *kisses him again, starts untying him, kissing him over and over.*)

NEWT: I'm married.

BECKY: I bet you jabber on 'n on about bein' married when you cheat on Penny.

NEWT: Go 'head. Untie me.

BECKY: Naw… guess I'll reheat some chili instead. Maybe a lot of the fun is just in the imagining… huh?

(BECKY *exits. After a beat,* NEWT *thrashes and rocks… and tips himself over.*)

LIGHTS SNAP TO BLACK: <u>THE END</u>

Rangeland's Gone

Time: 1991

Locale: Holbrook, Arizona

Characters: CARLOS, 26
JOY LYNN, 22

The original version of *Rangeland's Gone* was first produced by
State University of New York at Fredonia on March 6, 1995.
The producing director was Thomas W. Loughlin. The play
was directed by Jeff McConnell with the following cast:

Carlos   James Giannavola
Joy Lynn   Tara Bialy

A revised version of *Rangeland's Gone* was first produced by
The Sun Valley Festival of New Western Drama in
Ketchum, Idaho, on May 24, 1997. The festival's producer
was Ed LaGrande. The play was directed by Susan Bailey
with the following cast:

Carlos   Steve D. Smith
Joy Lynn   Kristine Leslie

(Upstage is a slide projection of a 1991 Arizona license plate. A plush motel room: queen bed with a Colonial style headboard, two purple armchairs near a table. An athletic style suitcase is open on the bed. Next to the suitcase is a cassock and a padre hat. CARLOS opens a sack of burgers at the table. Also on the table is a bottle of Kessler's Whiskey and a plastic glass filled with whiskey and tap water. CARLOS is wearing jeans, boots, a Western snap shirt, and a gunbelt with a holstered pistol. Next to the bed is a nightstand with a telephone. After a few bites, CARLOS goes to the phone, dials it, waits….)

CARLOS: Wake-up call… at eight. Yes, eight. Thank you. Bless you, son. *(He hangs up, returns to his food. He puts his feet up on the other chair, takes a drink of his whiskey ditch, shuts his eyes, enjoys the moment. Then he takes off his cowboy boots. He returns to his sack of food, extracts a bag of fries. There is a knock on the door. He is startled.)* Yes?

JOY LYNN: *(Offstage.)* Father, can I see you?

CARLOS: *(Checks his pistol, stands, calls out.)* It's late, child.

JOY LYNN: *(Offstage.)* It's an emergency.

CARLOS: *(Rushing into his cassock.)* But this isn't my parish.

JOY LYNN: *(Offstage.)* Life 'n death!

CARLOS: *(Buttons the cassock.)* Please wait.

JOY LYNN: (*Offstage.*) Hurry, Father.

CARLOS: Yes, yes… (*He exits.*)

JOY LYNN: (*Offstage.*) I need to confess.

CARLOS: (*Offstage.*) It's late, young lady. You should see the parish priest.

JOY LYNN: (*Offstage.*) I can't remember the words to say. It's been a few years.

CARLOS: (*Offstage.*) Come in for a few moments.

(CARLOS *and* JOY LYNN *enter. She is wearing a floppy leather hat, a low-cut pink-red top, and a black velvet mini-skirt, with sandals. Her clothes are sweat-stained and wet. Desert-slender, her hair is wild, unbrushed, and her face is red… brawl-bruised.*)

JOY LYNN: You must hate it… when people burst in on you.

CARLOS: Have a chair. Mind if I eat? (*He watches her hesitate.*) Go ahead. Sit down.

JOY LYNN: Remember me? From Burger King? I served you yesterday, Father.

CARLOS: Drive-thru window? What can I do for you? (*Picks up a burger.*)

JOY LYNN: Look, Father. I ain't gonna hard-sell my sins to you. If you'd rather it, I'll take off. But then this guy's gonna kill me.

CARLOS: (*Sets down the burger.*) What guy? He follow you?

JOY LYNN: He's gonna look for me. But right now he's at the hospital. So I got to leave. But I got no money.

CARLOS: Hardship comes from too much pride. (*They stare at each other for a beat or two.*) That's harsh. But that's what Jesus reckoned at the Last Supper.

JOY LYNN: Look, I got big trouble. You gonna help or not?

CARLOS: What exactly have you done?

JOY LYNN: It's what Duane did first.

CARLOS: Husband or boyfriend?

JOY LYNN: All but married.

CARLOS: I see.

JOY LYNN: He came at me like a rabies wolf, droolin'. Right outta his sleep. Woke up… woke me up. Grabbed my neck 'n hit me. Hit me 'n hit me.

CARLOS: Why?

JOY LYNN: It was like he spoke to himself in a dream… as if he dream-said to himself, "First thing I'm gonna do when I wake up is slug Joy Lynn."

CARLOS: He should be here for confession, not you.

JOY LYNN: I stuck him with a nail file.

CARLOS: That isn't too bad.

JOY LYNN: Stuck him in his <u>balls</u>.

CARLOS: *(Pause.)* I see your side of this.

JOY LYNN: People change, don't they. Like Duane.

CARLOS: Do you love him?

JOY LYNN: I'm wide-open to him.

CARLOS: But do you love him?

JOY LYNN: Couples tame-up each other, don't they? They surrender, right? Leave behind other stuff and other people? Put "No Trespassing" signs on each other. But what happens if one, or maybe both, at the same time, get jealous? Jealous makes it better. That's what a friend says. She says if there ain't jealousy, there ain't love.

CARLOS: Drink?

JOY LYNN: Guess you priests have to drink. No sex 'n all.

CARLOS: You can suppose that. (*He exits to find a plastic glass.*)

JOY LYNN: I cheated on Duane. Yesterday.

CARLOS: (*He returns, hands her a glass, pours a little whiskey into it.*) Tap water?

JOY LYNN: But he started it. Duane did it when we was both takin' courses at N.P.C.

CARLOS: N.P.C.?

JOY LYNN: The college. Duane cheated there.

CARLOS: I think it was over right then.

JOY LYNN: Not really. The more I shut him down, the more he harassed me.

CARLOS: How? (*No response.*) Sex.

JOY LYNN: Funny. The more he cheated, more he wanted to plank me. Like some wild hope it'd go back to what took us up together. (*Pause.*) So… you can forgive me for jabbin' the nail file into his balls?

CARLOS: Yes.

JOY LYNN: Okay. Then say the forgivin' words.

CARLOS: Make the sign of the cross.

JOY LYNN: (*Crosses herself.*) Okay.

CARLOS: God forgives you. Amen.

JOY LYNN: I'm the one who's supposed to say, "Amen," right?

CARLOS: Either way works. (*Pause.*) Glad I could help.

JOY LYNN: I still got a problem. Duane's gonna come lookin' for me. He said so. He said he's gonna smash my head in. So I have to leave Holbrook. Soon. (*Pause.*) And I am broke.

CARLOS: I can give you enough for a bus ticket.

JOY LYNN: He'll hunt me at the bus station.

CARLOS: Maybe you'll make up with him.

JOY LYNN: No. I'm all closed-up to him now.

CARLOS: I have a hundred dollars I can give you. (*Goes to his suitcase.*)

JOY LYNN: More than money, I need a <u>ride</u>. Duane's gonna be psycho.

CARLOS: Get a friend to take you.

JOY LYNN: I hear there's a women's shelter in Flagstaff. Duane will twist my friends… scramble faces. You don't know Duane. He don't make threats. You're a priest. You're supposed to help women like me. You can't glide out a this. I'm more than just broke. I'm massacred. What kind of priest are you? A sixty-five buck room in the Arizonian. Likely drivin' new wheels. Sittin' here with whiskey and a sack of food and the movie channel on TV. What's a hundred dollars to me? Just enough money for Duane to catch me… to break my legs so I can't squat to pee. (*Pause.*) You a fag priest? Like if I was a little boy, would you give me a ride? That it? You got a crippled heart? You get altar boys to suck you off? (*No response… pause.*) Do I got to beg?

Okay… I am begging. Hide me tonight. I can sleep in the chair. I won't bother you. Just give me a ride to even Winslow. Winslow. Please. Don't let Duane track me down, please!

CARLOS: (*Returns the twenty-dollar bills to his suitcase.*) Only as far as Winslow.

(JOY LYNN *rushes* CARLOS, *embraces him, leaps back away from him.*)

JOY LYNN: A gun! I felt a gun. What's a priest doin' with a gun?

CARLOS: What gun?

JOY LYNN: Under your priest clothes.

CARLOS: The gun… even priests get robbed.

JOY LYNN: (*Trying to circumnavigate him.*) When you last say Mass?

CARLOS: Sunday.

JOY LYNN: You ain't no priest. Priests say Mass every morning.

CARLOS: *(Flips her onto the bed, covers her mouth with his hand.)* Scream and I will poke your eyes out. *(Pause.)* Good. Don't fight it. Go with it. I will let you go in a second. Understand? *(He moves his hand off her mouth.)* You made a wish. It's come true. You get to sleep in the chair.

JOY LYNN: *(Goes to the chair.)* Who the hell are you?

CARLOS: I sleep light. You make for the door just once, just once, I'll finish you off with my bare hands.

JOY LYNN: Should a taken your money

CARLOS: Yeah. Go to sleep.

JOY LYNN: Can I have some whiskey?

CARLOS: Help yourself. But keep quiet.

JOY LYNN: *(Pours herself a drink.)* Someone's trying to catch you. *(No response. She watches him take off his cassock.)* They're gonna get you. You left that padre hat on the bed. Leavin' a hat on a bed is real bad luck.

CARLOS: No luck is your luck right now.

JOY LYNN: How's that?

CARLOS: (*Unsnaps his cowboy shirt, pulls it off.*) Keep drinkin'. Get drunk… make it easier for me tonight.

JOY LYNN: What'd you do? Murder? Burglary? (*Pause.*) Someone's gonna tell Duane they seen me come here.

CARLOS: Seventy rooms in this motel. He gonna knock all the doors? If he knocks on this door, I'll call the desk… have his ass arrested. (*He puts his suitcase on the floor, takes off his gunbelt, places it under the blankets.*)

JOY LYNN: What's your name?

CARLOS: Father Carlos Wade.

JOY LYNN: Carlos, baby, you just kidnapped me.

CARLOS: (*Gets into bed.*) Shut up.

JOY LYNN: Hope you sleep with one eye open. (*She takes a drink. She waits. After a beat, she bolts for the door.*) Bye.

CARLOS: (*He tackles her, drags her back, his hand over her mouth.*) You got no invite into my life. None. I tried to give you money. Leave me a choice, will you? Most men in my situation kill witnesses. Get it? You're a witness now. Have some common sense. Get up on the fucking bed! Now! (*He pulls her sandals off and tosses them under the table.*) Strip! Get those clothes off!

JOY LYNN: Don't hurt me.

CARLOS: Off! Your clothes stink! (*He yanks the bedspread off.*) Wrap yourself in this if you're modest. Make a bedroll out of it.

JOY LYNN: Come on, man. Tell me what to do. Just let me go.

CARLOS: Get your clothes off… or I'll rip 'em off.

JOY LYNN: (*She takes off her blouse and skirt.*) Far as I go.

CARLOS: Wrap the bedspread 'round you if you want. Then lie down next to me. On the table side.

(CARLOS *gets into bed.* JOY LYNN, *with the bedspread around her, lies down next to him.*)

CARLOS: I'll leave you in Winslow tomorrow. With a hundred dollars. Be grateful and go to sleep. Don't be a fool. Don't pull nothin'.

JOY LYNN: (*Pause.*) Carlos? My name is Joy Lynn Murphy. Just in case.

CARLOS: Goodnight, Joy Lynn. Good fucking night.

JOY LYNN: Please, don't be mean. We're both caught... in this room. You with what-all you've done... me with... with guilt.

CARLOS: You ain't guilty of nothin'.

JOY LYNN: This bed is nice. Much better 'n the one we have at the Sandman Motel over on West Hopi. Not much to rent in Holbrook. We got it on the weekly rate. Three-hundred a month. (*Pause.*) I'm an Air Force brat. Been about everywhere. Vegas was my favorite. A whole town lit up twenty-four hours. You ever been to Vegas? (*Pause.*) I'm scared, Carlos. Talk to me. I'm scared shitless. This is too intimate, you know? You ain't tellin' what you're feelin'. Can you feel me quiver? Please say something. Tell me you'll kill me. Or tell me I got to give you a blow job. Or tell me you like your women better stacked, that my boobs are way too small. Tell me if you're a diamondback. (*Pause.*) Carlos, I'll agree to anything. Want me to take off the rest of my clothes? Carlos, you gonna kill me out on the desert? Huh?

CARLOS: Don't shake. It'll be okay.

JOY LYNN: I can feel my life flyin' away from me.

CARLOS: (*Pause.*) Never lived in town. I grew up in the Texas Panhandle. We buried Momma when I was fifteen. God-forsaken ground. Poor grass. No good. Face-stingin'

96

wind. Got used to Beechnut chew early. (*He sits up. She sits up.*) I love this country, this West. But.... See: the rangeland's gone. What is left of it is becoming <u>agri-business</u>, pesticide-herbicide and cancer. Water no man can drink. (*Pause.*) But they left us our fillin' stations to rob.

JOY LYNN: You rob gas stations? That's what you do?

CARLOS: It was my dream. I'm livin' it out.

JOY LYNN: Then what?

CARLOS: (*Laughs.*) I'll own a map with 48 red circles on it. One for each hold-up. I have robbed seventeen fillin' stations in seventeen states. Crazy, ain't it? Like the padre disguise for between towns. But now the disguise has me in trouble... with you.

JOY LYNN: (*Slowly stands, as if testing him.*) Ain't any money in that kind of crime.

CARLOS: But it's an achievement... if I can do it. (*Pause.*) You ain't too thin for me, girl. (*Pause.*) Look: if they catch me <u>after</u> I knock down all forty-eight states, then I can write a book and sell it to the movies. That'll be worth a million. I don't know if my motive is money or fame... maybe it's the fame.

JOY LYNN: (*She takes off her bra and panties… puts on his cassock.*) You want fame… more than money?

CARLOS: America is 'bout tryin' for a million bucks. You know, I got a snapshot of all the places I took down. Good notes on each robbery, too. (*He pulls the suitcase onto the bed, opens it, gets out a small photo album.*) Lemme show you. First fillin' station I robbed was in Edmond, Oklahoma. My Daddy was gut-bleedin' to death in a hospital. Nothin' I could do. Our ranch was good as gone.

JOY LYNN: How am I in your disguise?

CARLOS: You look real good.

JOY LYNN: (*She takes his photo album to the table, sits with it.*) Thanks.

CARLOS: (*Stands, gets the money out of the suitcase.*) I want you to have the money, Joy Lynn. I'll take you to Winslow in the morning. (*Pause.*) Maybe my padre costume between robberies is changin' me. Thing is: I try to be moral.

JOY LYNN: You ever use your gun?

CARLOS: Shoot it? Naw. Seems I can pick the right fillin' station, the right shift, the right guy to rob. Instinct. Gut feeling. (*Pause.*) Don't laugh, but I can see myself ridin' with the real outlaws, Jesse James and them.

JOY LYNN: What about going home… back to your family ranch?

CARLOS: And buy it back? Last I heard, a funnel cloud ripped our house apart.

JOY LYNN: We won't ever see each other again, will we?

CARLOS: (*Pause.*) We should have a whiskey… 'n get some sleep.

(CARLOS *pours whiskey for both of them, hands her a glass, hold his glass up.*)

JOY LYNN: Make a toast!

CARLOS: To living wild!

JOY LYNN: To this night!

(*They drink.* JOY LYNN *laughs.*)

CARLOS: What?

JOY LYNN: Duane with my nail file stabbin' his nuts.

CARLOS: You're gonna phone him from Winslow, won't you?

JOY LYNN: You think so?

CARLOS: It's common.

JOY LYNN: I ain't so common. I don't know. Sure ain't eager for Duane to punch my lights out. (*Pause.*) You must have a low opinion of me if you think I'm gonna settle for Duane… for all that crap. (*She puts her glass down and takes his glass and puts it down, too.*) But I don't know if I can sleep with you, Carlos. I don't know. You got this half-forgotten West of outlaws. I got a city lust, like with Vegas, with ol' 24-hour Las Vegas.

(JOY LYNN *takes* CARLOS' *hand, starts to lead him in a waltz, starts to softly sing a song like "Waltz Across Texas." They waltz.*)

LIGHTS SNAP TO BLACK: <u>THE END</u>

This Is Dead Level

Time: 1994

Locale: Ely, Nevada

Characters: ALVIN BLACKHORSE, 44
THORA GREEN, 37
ELDON LETT, 65
WENDY FENTON, 35

This Is Dead Level was first produced by State University of New York at Fredonia on March 6, 1995. The producing director was Thomas W. Loughlin. The play was directed by Peter Dimas with the following cast:

Alvin   Christopher Thompson
Thora   Mary Regan
Eldon   Matt Osterhaus
Wendy   Lauren Vollette

(*A motel room at the Copper Queen. ALVIN is on his back, crossways, on the bed, his head on THORA'S lap. He is wearing jockey shorts. THORA is sitting on the bed, with her feet on the floor. She's in panties and bra.*)

THORA: A silver ring would be nice.

ALVIN: Think so?

THORA: Sure. I liked 'em when I was her age.

ALVIN: They're cheap?

THORA: You won't put out much.

ALVIN: I want to get her somethin' to make up for all this time.

THORA: (*Pause.*) It's been nice, sugar. But I gotta go.

ALVIN: You think I can get her a nice silver ring?

THORA: Absolutely. (*Pause.*) Come on, baby, raise up your head.

ALVIN: (*Lifts his head, moves.*) You could help pick it out.

THORA: (*Stands.*) I wish I could. (*Starts to get her skirt and blouse.*) But good luck.

103

ALVIN: How long you been a sporty?

THORA: (*Dressing.*) There's a jewelry store downtown. Check it out.

ALVIN: You never even said your name.

THORA: I work under the name a "Dawn."

ALVIN: How much for an afternoon?

THORA: To help you pick a ring?

ALVIN: Yeah.

THORA: I don't do that.

ALVIN: Another hun'red?

THORA: You got that much?

ALVIN: A bit more 'n that.

THORA: Sorry. I make it a rule: nothing unprofessional.

ALVIN: You might consider it like branchin' out, Dawn. (*Pause.*) Then how about another fuck? Straight in. Hun'red?

THORA: You ready again?

ALVIN: Could be.

THORA: I got to phone in first.

ALVIN: Call in.

THORA: Like I know you must be short a money 'n all.

ALVIN: I like your style.

THORA: Money first.

ALVIN: (*Finds his wallet in his jeans.*) This buys an hour, right?

THORA: If you can go that long, sugar. (*Pause.*) Yeah... an hour. I didn't mean that as an insult or anything.

ALVIN: That's okay. I got a car. We can take the second half hour to go to that jewelry store.

THORA: You don't have no car, And if you did, it's against rules for me to get into a car with you.

ALVIN: You could drive us. You're allowed to pick up hitchhikers? I could hitch a ride. Then you wouldn't be in a car with a customer. (*He holds out five twenty-dollar bills.*)

105

THORA: (*Takes the money, sticks it into her purse.*) You wanna do it in front of the mirror this time? (*She takes off her blouse, tosses it onto a chair.*)

ALVIN: (*Goes to her, undoes her skirt, lets it fall to the floor.*) Guess our first time was too ordinary. But I was hemmed-in for a couple years… and needed it quick.

THORA: We can do it just an itty-bitty more ruffianistic. Or showy.

(*There is a knock on the door.*)

ALVIN: That someone for you?

THORA: No. But I better call in.

ALVIN: I don't know anybody here in Ely.

THORA: Probably the maid. (*More knocking on the door.*) Get the door… 'n I'll call in. Then I'll do ya.

ALVIN: (*Goes to the door, opens it a crack*) What the fuck ya want?

ELDON: (*Offstage.*) Thora still here?

ALVIN: Go away, old man.

THORA: I'm here, Eldon. Let him in, okay?

(ALVIN *lets in* ELDON, *who is in a rumpled old suit.*)

ELDON: Thora, ol' Spunky is dyin'.

ALVIN: Who is this geezer?

ELDON: They think it's a stroke.

THORA: Oh, Eldon, I'm sorry. (*She hugs* ELDON.)

ELDON: He's getting summoned by the Lord.

ALVIN: I kind a like to be seduced right now, but the mood here is bummin' me out.

THORA: (*To* ALVIN.) I'm real sorry. This is my stepdad. I'll give back your money.

ALVIN: I don't want my money back.

ELDON: I can wait outside. Ain't you done it yet?

THORA: Eldon, can you wait in my car? I'll give you the keys, okay?

ELDON: Spunky will be dead by then.

ALVIN: Who the hell is Spunky?

THORA: His wife. Look… Mister…

ALVIN: Alvin.

THORA: Alvin, I've never done this before to a client, but I'm gonna give your money back to you. (*She retrieves her purse.*)

ALVIN: Hold on. He said this person is a <u>he</u>. One of you is lyin' to me.

ELDON: Spunky's my dog. Part Lab. Twelve years old. Thora lied so's we can just get outta here. You can understand that, can't ya?

THORA: He's close to that dog. It's all he's got.

ALVIN: Yeah. But right now, lady, you're all <u>I've</u> got. Plus I'm paid-up. (*A knock on the door.*) Damn, who you got after you this time, lady?

ELDON: I tol' Shirley I was comin' to get you.

THORA: Shirley's his girlfriend. They hang out at the Seniors' Center.

(ALVIN *goes to the door, opens it, and a giant bunny rabbit walks in… holding a tray of breakfast food and an envelope.*)

WENDY: (*Dressed as a bunny rabbit.*) Alvin Blackhorse?

ALVIN: That's me.

WENDY: Today is your lucky day!

ALVIN: No, it ain't.

THORA: (*Steering* ELDON *toward the door.*) Bye. I'll be back in an hour, okay?

ALVIN: (*Blocking* ELDON *and* THORA *from leaving.*) Lemme jaw with you a bit over this!

WENDY: Alvin Blackhorse, your Easter Egg is the Winner!

ALVIN: What Easter Egg?

WENDY: The First Annual Easter Egg Dash for Cash 'n Prizes.

ELDON: Thora, can you spot me ten bucks for some tangle-leg?

ALVIN: I'll take the cash. You keep any prize that ain't gonna become cash.

WENDY: First you gotta get back into bed for the free breakfast.

(ALVIN *drags* THORA *to the bed, forces her down on it.*)

ALVIN: Give the breakfast to Mrs. Blackhorse here.

ELDON: (*To* THORA.) You married him?

THORA: Eldon, sit down a minute, will ya?

WENDY: (*Serving* THORA *the breakfast tray.*) But I have to present the envelope. (*Takes the envelope, then, to* ALVIN.) On behalf of the Copper Queen Casino and Motel... the Grand Prize!

(WENDY *faints.*)

ELDON: She's had a stroke!

ALVIN: (*Pulls the rabbit head off* WENDY.) Lady, hey, lady! (*To* THORA.) She's pourin' sweat.

THORA: (*Picks up a link of sausage.*) I ain't had nothin' to eat all day.

(ALVIN *unzips the rabbit costume, strips it off* WENDY, *then starts to take off her sweat-soaked waitress outfit, too.*)

ELDON: Thora, I told the vet I'd be right back. He'll work on Spunky for charity, but I need whiskey.

THORA: (*Hands a piece of toast to* ELDON.) Here.

ELDON: Vet thinks it's a stroke. With brain surgery, there ain't no margin for errors.

(ALVIN *drags the half-conscious* WENDY *to the bed.*)

THORA: Alvin, open her envelope. See what you won.

WENDY: (*Soft moan.*) I feel bad.

THORA: (*An arm around* WENDY.) Alvin, get a damp washcloth.

ELDON: (*Picks up the envelope as* ALVIN *exits for a washcloth.*) Hot damn, maybe the day's not all lost. I should get a taste a this for bringin' him luck.

ALVIN: (*Back with a washcloth.*) Old man, gimme that envelope. (*Receives the envelope and slowly opens it.*)

WENDY: That you, Thora?

THORA: Yeah, Wendy, it's me.

WENDY: This is so embarrassing.

THORA: (*Wipes* WENDY'S *brow.*) Feel like some orange juice. You done sweated a whole lake.

(WENDY *sips orange juice.*)

ALVIN: What's 250 pulls on the Quartermania worth?

THORA: When you gotta use the pulls?

ALVIN: Today. By check-out time. Noon.

WENDY: I'd feel better if I was back to whorin'. I ain't getting' back into that goddamned bunny outfit again.

ELDON: I'll buy those 250 Quartermania pulls from ya… for, say, thirty-dollars.

ALVIN: (*To* WENDY.) They got a particular slot machine I gotta use?

WENDY: Yeah.

ELDON: Thora, loan me thirty bucks.

ALVIN: Your name's Thora, huh? (*Pause.*) Thora, let's go get that silver ring.

WENDY: (*To* THORA.) You married <u>him</u>?

THORA: He's got this thing… wants me to help him pick out some ring for his daughter.

ELDON: You won't win squat on that machine. But I got the touch.

ALVIN: Shut up, old man.

ELDON: How's about we go partners? That way I can pay the vet. I hate charity. This is dead level: I once whupped them machines for five-grand in one day. Ask Thora. Happened when I was married to her late mother. They banned me from gamblin' for five years after that. We go partners, you'll come out ahead.

WENDY: (*To* ALVIN.) Got a daughter? Really?

ALVIN: Over near Hawthorne. Yeah. Ain't seen her in a while.

WENDY: Thora, you ought to go with him. Big boy, how long they have you in the joint?

ALVIN: Seven years.

WENDY: (*Picks up half a grapefruit.*) That's too bad, Alvin.

ALVIN: Do the crime… sometimes do the time. (*Pause.*)
Old man, you gotta go. (ALVIN *takes out his wallet and hands*
ELDON *a twenty dollar bill.*)

ELDON: I wouldn't a bothered you, but Spunky had the
frothy mouth. Could a been rabies. But it was a stroke. (*To*
THORA.) Can I take supper at your place tonight?

THORA: (*To* ALVIN.) I better go. Take your money back.

ALVIN: Only if you go to the jewelry store with me.

WENDY: Thora, you give him his money… and I'll do the
actualities for him.

THORA: That okay, Alvin? Wendy will get you back into a
lovin' mood.

WENDY: I'm good as fired-up anyway. And I'd go to the
jewelry store, too. What was you in for anyway?

ALVIN: You're gonna help pick out a ring, too?

(THORA *and* ELDON *exit.*)

ALVIN: Hey, she left with my money.

WENDY: Relax. I know where to find her.

ALVIN: Want to shower first?

WENDY: After.

ALVIN: Okay. *(He stands… doesn't move… looks at the bunny costume.)*

WENDY: *(Caresses his face.)* Something wrong, baby? *(Pause.)* Want to do it with me in the Easter Bunny get-up? With or without the bunny head?

ALVIN: What your name?

WENDY: What it says on the tag on my waitress costume: Wendy. Wendy Fenton. Married just once. You need to know anything else?

ALVIN: And what was her real name?

WENDY: Thora Green. And that was Eldon Lett. They's married.

ALVIN: No.

WENDY: Okay, no. His dog have a stroke again? Thora punched her beeper alarm. So Eldon showed up. You spooked her.

(ALVIN *picks up the rabbit outfit, half zips it back up, begins stuffing the bedspread into it, then the blanket.* WENDY *helps. They stuff the outfit… arrange the stuffed rabbit on the bed.*)

ALVIN: I sort of liked her. I'll get over it.

WENDY: Thora's okay 'n all, but nothin' special. Me… I can be real special. Thora and I worked the same brothel for a time. You'll like me better.

ALVIN: I don't mean all that. I mean asking names. I ask names too much.

WENDY: Names are a kind of navigation.

(*They force a pillow or two into the rabbit head, then set it atop the stuffed rabbit torso.*)

ALVIN: Names are just some kind a fanfare. Kinds of tattooed-on things. It's what people do… what people whisper to each other at night. You understand?

WENDY: (*She puts the envelope and the prize certificate on the rabbit's torso.*) Today is your lucky day, Alvin Blackhorse.

(*They half-waltz, kiss.*)

LIGHTS SNAP TO BLACK: <u>THE END</u>

Farewell the Catastrophe Works

Time: 1994

Locale: Las Vegas, Nevada

Characters: FIONA, 58
             MARJORIE, 28, Fiona's daughter

Farewell the Catastrophe Works was first produced by University of Nevada, Las Vegas, on October 5, 1990. It was directed by Maggie Winn-Jones with the following cast:

Fiona   Gina Torrecilla
Marjorie   Laura Tompkins

(Upstage is a royal blue banner with silver script, proclaiming, "Loan Office / First National Gaming Bank of Nevada." Downstage of that banner is a wonderful desk and its chair, plus another chair for customers. MARJORIE is busily sorting papers. After a moment, FIONA enters, pushing a loaded-up shopping cart. MARJORIE is horrified.)

MARJORIE: Oh my god.

FIONA: Hello, honey.

MARJORIE: What're you doing here?

FIONA: Give me a peck.

MARJORIE: You're supposed to be…

FIONA: Home?

MARJORIE: Yes.

FIONA: I need a small holiday.

MARJORIE: Why didn't you phone?

FIONA: Well, aren't I worth a peck on the cheek?

MARJORIE: Mother!

FIONA: Say the word and I'll leave. I will.

MARJORIE: Oh god.

(MARJORIE *stands and leads* FIONA *to the chair for customers, but does not kiss her.*)

FIONA: Your cage rattled?

MARJORIE: But…

FIONA: The sporting goods factory closed down.

MARJORIE: Oh no.

FIONA: So I decided…

MARJORIE: Yes?

FIONA: I haven't had breakfast yet, honey. Could you send out for something?

(MARJORIE *opens a desk drawer and takes out a bowl filled with lollypops.* FIONA *takes the bowl and empties it into her lap and hands back the bowl.*)

MARJORIE: When it rains….

FIONA: If you had married Doyle, I wouldn't have had such a miserable journey.

MARJORIE: Mother, I'll phone and get you into a motel. Then you have to go home.

FIONA: Because the man you married hates me.

MARJORIE: Jim does not hate you.

FIONA: He does so. I smelled it on his breath. Pepper breath covered with cheap mints.

MARJORIE: (*Picks up the phone.*) I will not have another of your scenes.

FIONA: My scenes? (*She stands.*) Forget it. I'll just wander off. There's so much to do in this city. I read the travel leaflets on the train. Then I used them to wipe myself. That colored ink takes care of....

MARJORIE: Okay, no motel. (*Puts down the phone.*) But only one night at the house.

FIONA: Doyle always liked me. You should have married him. He valued my experiences.

MARJORIE: This is no place for you.

FIONA: There is no place for me, Marjorie.

MARJORIE: What have you done?

FIONA: It's what the world has done to me.

MARJORIE: Do you have a return ticket?

FIONA: Ticket?

MARJORIE: Yes. You had to have tickets to get out here.

FIONA: Not me. I pushed that shopping cart all the way here. All the way from Manitowish Waters. I slept under old copies of The Daily Globe. As the weather got warmer—it warms up the further south you go—I threw away newspapers.

MARJORIE: Please, mother.

FIONA: You don't believe me.

MARJORIE: Exactly.

FIONA: Okay, I took the train.

MARJORIE: So you do have a ticket home?

FIONA: Not at all.

MARJORIE: What in the world did you have in mind? (*Pause.*) Fine. Jim and I will pay your way home.

FIONA: I told you. There is no home.

MARJORIE: You have a house still, don't you? (*No response.*) What did you do?

FIONA: I said, "Farewell the catastrophe works." That is what I did.

MARJORIE: Mother, lay it out, please.

FIONA: You should've married Doyle. His father and I shared a special moment.

MARJORIE: Not Dillinger again.

FIONA: Doyle's father was there with me the day Dillinger shot it out with the FBI boys.

MARJORIE: (*Picks up the phone.*) Please stay with us, mother. I'll call a taxi. You can...

FIONA: My shopping cart won't fit into a taxi.

MARJORIE: (*Puts down the phone.*) Please... make sense.

FIONA: The day was April 22, 1934. Doyle's daddy and I were bringing food to Baby Face Nelson and Dillinger and…

MARJORIE: Mother, you were only two years old. I don't want to listen to this again.

FIONA: Then how come I remember it so vivid? Tell me that.

MARJORIE: What did you do with our house?

FIONA: <u>Our</u> house? Listen here, I was there and it was Doyle's daddy and I who hid Dillinger and Nelson on the Lac Du Flambeau Indian Reservation.

MARJORIE: Enough!

FIONA: *(She goes to the cart and deposits the lollypops into a sack. Then she takes out a rusty, pocked-barrel revolver.)* I could rob this bank, you know.

MARJORIE: Mother, put that away!

FIONA: How about a loan?

MARJORIE: Put the gun away!

FIONA: It doesn't work.

MARJORIE: For Christ sake, put it away!

FIONA: It belonged to Doyle's grandfather. He came out West. Do you remember?

MARJORIE: Mother, have you ever wondered why I left home?

FIONA: He worked on the old Goodnight Trail. He was a scout. They used to send him ahead to talk reason to the sodbusters, as they moved big herds of cattle north. See, the sodbusters always tried to charge a lot for water for the cows. Especially in Kansas. Water is a free item in this world. Grandpa Doyle was sent ahead with his gun. This very gun.

MARJORIE: Put the gun away… or else!

FIONA: *(Places the revolver in her cart.)* Make me a loan.

MARJORIE: No. I cannot do that.

FIONA: I have a plan.

MARJORIE: No.

FIONA: I'm going to organize specialty acts for rodeo shows.

MARJORIE: *(Finds her purse.)* I am going to give you all the money in my purse. And that will be the end of my obligation. Do you understand that?

FIONA: You're so like your father.

MARJORIE: You hated my father.

FIONA: Not true. But imagine this: National Anthem singers on horseback, cowboy monkeys, poodles riding horses, a topless girl matador, trick roping…. This will be a class pageantry kind of thing. Dancing horses, a buffalo that leaps through a flaming hoop…

MARJORIE: Cowboy monkeys.

FIONA: That's a real winner of an act. They ride working border collies that move calves around the arena.

MARJORIE: Mother, I'm sorry…

FIONA: You're sorry?

MARJORIE: Yes, mother, I am sorry that we kept sending you Christmas cards.

FIONA: *(Pause.)* It's your father's fault.

MARJORIE: Because I like to inflict pain?

FIONA: He taught you that.

MARJORIE: Because he took me to see the Sioux Sun Dance.

FIONA: That's right. I told him, I said, "Harold, take Marjorie to that dude ranch for kids, but no stops along the way.

MARJORIE: You don't have a bit of information on that, not accurate information.

FIONA: Just the pain part.

MARJORIE: (*Dumps out her purse on the desk.*) Here. Take what you wish.

FIONA: No, I have a gift for <u>you</u>. Actually, that's why I'm here. That is if I can't have the loan. (*Pause. She takes a funeral urn from the cart.*). These are your great grandfather's ashes.

MARJORIE: They are not! Those ashes are from my cat. You took them from my old bedroom and brought them here to torture me.

FIONA: No, the ashes you're thinking of are now buried behind our old house, which I sold, by the way, to pay off your college loan. (*Pause.*) That's right. I paid off your student loan. I couldn't bear to have Mr. Heavey keep asking me how you were getting along.

MARJORIE: I am up to date on payments!

FIONA: That's not what I heard.

MARJORIE: You're lying.

FIONA: Want me to find the pay-off papers?

MARJORIE: (*Pause.*) You deserved to have to pay it off.

FIONA: I did? How's that?

MARJORIE: Ever since Dad died, you made me pay rent.

FIONA: To teach you how money works.

MARJORIE: You played bingo with it. And you gave it away to Doyle to date me!

FIONA: That was to the good, wasn't it?

MARJORIE: Do you think I had fun as Doyle asked for receipts when we went to the movie house? Or out to the café?

FIONA: So you run off to South Dakota to marry a…

MARJORIE: I married a school teacher.

FIONA: Make me a loan. Forget about Jim. Let bygones be bygones. I put some of my own money into getting you dated properly, to make sure you ate good food after movies. I even bought tires for Doyle's Buick. So make me a loan. (*Pause.*) No! I said to myself all the way here, listening to the clack-clack of the train, I said to myself, "Fiona, your little girl is still your little girl. There's time for us to get along, to understand each other."

MARJORIE: Mother, I am about to press the alarm button.

FIONA: You are?

MARJORIE: I am.

FIONA: You'd have your mother arrested?

MARJORIE: I will have you removed from the bank.

FIONA: And at the trial, I will have to testify to certain things, about your past, how I paid off your student loan… at the loss of my own home. (*Pause.*) Look, just take the urn and do me one favor and I'll leave.

MARJORIE: Oh god.

FIONA: Take the urn. Like I said, it has your great grandfather in it. Take it and walk it to Kilkenny.

MARJORIE: Walk it to Ireland?

FIONA: That is what I request.

MARJORIE: You can't walk to Ireland.

FIONA: Yes, you can. One step after another.

MARJORIE: You ought to do it.

FIONA: You walk it from here to New York. Then you catch a ship. And you walk the urn around the deck until you land in Ireland. Then you walk it to Kilkenny. We can trace our family back five thousand years. It's our ancestors who carved the Neolithic tomb at Newgrange! You owe it to us.

MARJORIE: Hand me the urn.

FIONA: Now you want it?

MARJORIE: Yes.

FIONA: To finally recognize me?

MARJORIE: Do you want me to do this thing for you or not?

FIONA: Jim is not going to allow you to walk the urn home to Ireland.

MARJORIE: I will do it.

(*Slowly* FIONA *rises and slowly she hands over the urn.* FIONA *goes to her shopping cart, starts to exit as* MARJORIE *watches.* FIONA *turns, blows her daughter a kiss, exits.* MARJORIE *looks inside the urn, takes out a small shard of bone, examines it in the palm of her hand, then drops it back into the urn.* Then she places the urn in her wastepaper can.* FIONA *runs back in, retrieves the urn.*)

FIONA: You gambled it was the cat, right? But it's your father.

(FIONA *returns the urn to the wastepaper can, then exits.* MARJORIE *kneels by the can.*)

LIGHTS SNAP TO BLACK: <u>THE END</u>

Red Shuttleworth

The Genuine Love of the Kid's Life

Time: 1881

Locale: Near Roswell, New Mexico

Characters: KID, 21, a pistolero
PAT, 30, a lawman
LOOKING GLASS, 17, a girl

The Genuine Love of the Kid's Life, under the title *The Great Western Land Pirate*, was first produced by the University of Nevada, Las Vegas, on May 9. 1991. It was directed by Davey Marlin-Jones with the following cast:

Kid   Todd Espeland
Pat   Bradley Goodwill
Looking Glass Toni Loppnow

A revised version of *The Genuine Love of the Kid's Life,* something close to this version, was first produced by the Sun Valley Festival of New Western Drama in Ketchum, Idaho, on May 24, 1997. Ed LeGrande was the producer of the festival. The play was directed by Cathy Reinheimer with the following cast:

Kid   Dean Rutherford
Pat   Chris Esparza
Looking Glass   Mary Kennedy

(Upstage are two abstract New Mexico landscape paintings… and a mobile featuring crude wooden directional signs for El Paso, Los Angeles, Santa Fe, and Chihuahua. Lights rise. The KID is in his camp. There's a coffee pot, a saddle, a bedroll, a couple of .41 caliber Colt double action revolvers atop an oil rag, a Winchester 44.40 rifle in a scabbard, a sombrero, a Spanish dagger, a bottle of rye. The KID is wearing a dusty black frock coat, dark trousers, a vest over a pale shirt, and blunt-toed riding boots. He is looking at the cover of a dime novel. He reads the title aloud.)

KID: <u>The Great Western Land Pirate Or The Genuine Love of the Kid's Life</u>. *(Pause. He rubs the cover.)* Well, well, well… I'll be switched. A book about me. Even if it ain't but half true. *(He looks around, sees no one, opens the book.)* Guess I'll have another read of it. *(He reads aloud.)* "Billy the Kid made himself known and feared in that bloody land. A bold and brave and unscrupulous bandito, William H. Bonney was only seventeen in that year. When he smiled, strong men shook and chilled at the gleam of his ever-present smile. The kid had <u>fangs</u>." *(He drops the book.)* I don't have any fangs! My front teeth poke out a bit, but they ain't fangs. *(The KID laughs, but stops when he hears something approach. He rapidly conceals his weapons, except one Colt. He lies down, pretends to sleep.)*

PAT *(Offstage)* Kid, you there? Hey, Kid?

(PAT cautiously enters, but with his pistols holstered. He is well-dressed and wears <u>two</u> badges. He stops once he spots the KID, whose

hands are beneath a blanket, and whose head rests on a saddle with the sombrero over his face.)

PAT: Billy, I know you ain't dozin'.

KID: You don't know that. You don't know at all. I <u>might</u> be asleep.

PAT: Kid, I come a ways so we can talk.

KID: (*Sitting up.*) Coffee? It's cold, but I got some.

PAT: No thanks.

KID: (*Putting his pistols into holsters.*) I knew it was you, Pat. Knew the horse. That martingale makes it more different. I think it shortens the steps.

PAT: I don' think so.

KID: (*Pause.*) Fine. You can have that point. Anyways, I knew it was you. That's why I was relaxed.
PAT: With Colts in your hands relaxed.

KID: Aw, Pat, you'd never dry gulch me. You're no back-shooter.

PAT: Not yet anyways.

KID: (*Pause.*) Right. There's times for it. You hate back-drillin', but sometimes…. Actually, I prefer to fight it out cantina-style. Just ol' knuckles 'n skull.

PAT: But when you lose at fists…

KID: Then it's time for Mr. Colt.

PAT: (*Pause.*) That mouse-colored horse of yours is well-rested, Kid. (*Pause.*) You could go a ways on her.

KID: If I had a notion to.

PAT: You might want to consider it.

KID: Pat, did you bring mezcal?

PAT: No. (*He pours himself some cold coffee.*)

KID: You get to see God with mezcal.

PAT: That's about right.
KID: When you eat the worm in the bottle bottom.

PAT: We did that…. Many times, huh, Billy?

KID: Many times. Did ya bring us two ladies?

PAT: Not this time.

138

KID: Sometimes I think I ought to settle-up with Deluvina Maxwell.

PAT: Nice girl.

KID: But afterwards, you know, she spooks me.

PAT: That so.

KID: When she whispers, "Duerme bien Querido."

PAT: Sleep well, beloved.

KID: What would <u>you</u> do if some girl whispered <u>that</u> to you? Pat, that's words to scratch onto a grave marker.

PAT: She might get to do it yet.

KID: And then there's Flora Korkus.

PAT: Schoolmarm in Roswell.
KID: Pat, why didn't you bring us out some girls, for just you 'n me, like the old days?

PAT: Not this time.

KID: You got badges pinned on this time.

PAT: Funny twist for me.

KID: That the new John Chisum plan? Get all the rustlers to wear badges?

PAT: The old days are over.

KID: Two badges, though?

PAT: (*Points to the badges in turn.*) This badge says I'm the county sheriff. And this one says I'm a Deputy United States Marshal.

KID: You're sure mobbed-up with the law.

PAT: The old days are gone.

KID: Well, that Nellie Pickett is the nicest.

PAT: You gonna kill a friend to get his wife?

KID: Naw… not likely. But Nellie is the nicest. You'd probably help me get her out of this country.

PAT: I might, if you were to really leave.

KID: You don't much like her, do you?

PAT: I'm not the one who wants to couple with her.

KID: True. But you said something about Nellie once.

PAT: Nellie dresses with barbaric richness.

KID: She likes me.

PAT: Damnedest thing.

KID: She says out in Australia they got an animal that can prizefight.

PAT: Kangaroo.

KID: I says to her, "Nellie, maybe one of these years I'll take you over the ocean to see it." I says to her, "You can watch me fight it."

PAT: Do it, Billy. Do it.

KID: A possible, huh?
PAT: Catch a coach to California. Then a ship.

KID: So many borders to cross. How far is it?

PAT: Not far.

KID: (*Pause.*) No mezcal and no girls, Pat.

141

PAT: Not today.

KID: We could go rustle some Chisum cow-calf pairs.

PAT: Not today.

KID: Want to try 'n out-pull leather on me?

PAT: For fun and practice? Or for blood?

KID: Practice. No trigger jerkin'. Only a game for two ol' pals.

PAT: We could. To pass some time.

KID: You trust me not to shoot?

PAT: On your <u>word</u>? Always.

KID: If we agreed before.

PAT: That's right.

KID: (*Stands.*) You go first.

(*The sound of a branch snapping or of a stone being kicked.*)

PAT: What in Sam Hill?

(More noise from someone walking… someone shuffling along wearily.)

KID: Pat, this a set-up? You got a posse?

PAT: No.

KID: You been followed!

PAT: Absolutely not. I circled 'n circled… checked my trail.

(LOOKING GLASS, an attractive, coyote-lean girl, enters… dressed in men's clothing. In one hand she has a carpetbag loaded with clothes and photographic supplies. She is also dragging a box camera attached to a tripod. She shuffles into camp.)

KID: Where are the others?

LOOKING GLASS: *(She does not respond. She sets down her carpetbag, drags her camera/tripod toward the KID'S things.)*

LOOKING GLASS: Where's your water?
KID: *(Points to a canteen.)* How many with you? They dead? Apaches get 'em?

(LOOKING GLASS drinks until PAT takes the canteen from her.)

LOOKING GLASS: And I'm hungry, too.

PAT: Kid, what've you got?

KID: Chunk a dried venison is all.

(LOOKING GLASS *sits. The* KID *finds the venison and brings it to her.*)

PAT: Where's your man?

(LOOKING GLASS *begins to eat off the chunk of meat.*)

KID: I should a sliced her some meat. Now her spit is gonna be all over it. (*To her.*) Soon as you can, tell me where your people are.

LOOKING GLASS: (*Pause.*) Oakland.

PAT: Oakland where?

LOOKING GLASS: Oakland, California.

PAT: But who came with you?

LOOKING GLASS: It's just me.

KID: Miss, you don't know who you're talkin' to. I get straight answers.

LOOKING GLASS: Biscuits?

KID: My name is known the world-wide. I'm about as famous a desperado as there is.

PAT: Miss, we can help, but you have to tell us what went wrong.

LOOKING GLASS: Wrong?

KID: Pat, she ain't gonna tell <u>you</u>. I'm the famous one here.

LOOKING GLASS: Nothing is particularly wrong.

PAT: Miss, you can talk to me. I'm the sheriff. But I can't help if you don't talk. The others that came with you, if they're still alive, maybe I can reach 'em in time.

(*Silence for a beat.*)

KID: (*Holds out his hand.*) William H. Bonney at your service. (*Gets no response.*) But most folks know me as Billy the Kid.

(*Silence for a beat.*)

PAT: (*To the* KID.) Don't hawk her. She must've come across a band of Mescalero Apache. She's in shock.

KID: (*Shows* LOOKING GLASS *the dime novel.*) See this book. It's about me. (*No response… and a pause.*) Course the fellow on the cover ain't me. That's the thing about dime novels. They make 'em up. But it's me on the cover, even if it ain't me. See, it's <u>supposed</u> to be me.

PAT: Christ, another Billy the Kid dime novel.

KID: Yeah, Pat.

LOOKING GLASS: More water, please.

(PAT *starts to hand her the canteen, but the* KID *stops him.*)

KID: Sure. Water. But tell us your name first.

LOOKING GLASS: Kate.

KID: Last name? (*He gets no response.*) Look, I ain't tryin' to sell you a bible or tainted beef.
LOOKING GLASS: Kate's good enough for you.

(PAT *hands her the canteen and she drinks.*)

PAT: Kate, how'd you get here?

LOOKING GLASS: Soul travel.

(*The* KID *and* PAT *look at each other.*)

146

PAT: I can't rescue your folks if you don't help us out.

LOOKING GLASS: My name is Kate Tenney. I soul travelled here from Oakland, California.

KID: With a carpetbag and a box camera?

LOOKING GLASS: Is this Texas?

PAT: New Mexico. Lincoln County.

LOOKING GLASS: Are you certain?

KID: Last time we checked we were sure.

LOOKING GLASS: That's the only trouble with soul travel. You have to do it by daylight if you ain't been to that place before.

PAT: That place?

LOOKING GLASS: Texas.

KID: Well, well, well... I'll be switched. A girl with a camera soul goddamned travelin' to Texas.

(*The* KID *makes to touch her camera.*)

LOOKING GLASS: Don't touch it!

KID: Possessive, huh? (*Pause.*) If it's that important, I'm gonna name you after it: Looking Glass.

LOOKING GLASS: My name is <u>Kate</u> <u>Tenney</u>.

KID: Oh, no, not now. Now it's <u>Looking</u> <u>Glass</u>.

PAT: Kate, this is the frontier. So the kid figures we got the rights to name 'n rename everything.

LOOKING GLASS: I already have a name. (*She stands… as if to leave.*)

PAT: Where are you going?

LOOKING GLASS: Texas.

KID: What if you wind up in Colorado?
PAT: Better stay with us, Kate. You'll be safer.

LOOKING GLASS: Safer? With two madmen? In the middle of nowhere getting my name changed?

KID: Looking Glass has a nice ring to it.

LOOKING GLASS: A looking glass is a <u>mirror</u>. I am a photographer and my instrument is called a <u>camera</u>.

KID: You're sure a pistol, Looking Glass.

(LOOKING GLASS *starts to leave, but* PAT *stops her.*)

PAT: Hold on, Kate. Maybe you can help <u>us</u>.

LOOKING GLASS: Help you?

PAT: That's right.

KID: What's she gonna help with?

PAT: Me and the Kid have had a dispute. You judge the fairness of it.

KID: You can't lock me to that, Pat! What if she says I have to go off to the calaboose with you? You think I'll go for that? Then I'd have to pull-off one of my daring escapes again. (*Pause.*) I got a better notion, Looking Glass. You stick around 'n I'll read you this authentic true story of my life, which ain't at all true, but it's interesting.

LOOKING GLASS: No thank you, gentlemen.

KID: See, this book says I have fangs.

PAT: You get your fangs pulled by a dentist, Billy?

KID: Looking Glass, look at my teeth. (*He smiles.*) See? Look, you can touch 'em if you like.

149

PAT: Kid, you don't ask a lady to touch your teeth.

KID: Why not?

PAT: It's not good personal hygiene.

KID: I keep 'em clean. And I don't have a fang in my mouth. These books don't tell the complete truth. Looking Glass, you spend the night 'n I'll read it to you, and then you can tell everybody how Billy the Kid told you truth from lies.

LOOKING GLASS: I must be leaving.

KID: Who're you gonna meet who's more important than me?

LOOKING GLASS: (*Pause.*) I'm going to Texas to take pictures of Judge Roy Bean.

PAT: I've heard of him.

KID: I'm more famous.

LOOKING GLASS: No, you're not. I have never heard of you. On the other hand, Judge Roy Bean, who is fruitlessly in love with actress Lily Langtry…

KID: Aw, go 'head. Go.

PAT: Kid, no. She can help us with our dispute.

KID: You're gonna ask a soul-travelin' looking glass to be the one who decides.

LOOKING GLASS: (*To* PAT.) If it won't take too long. I really have to go. This time I'm heading in the right direction.

PAT: This time?

LOOKING GLASS: Last month I landed on a fishing boat off the coast of Ireland. You can imagine the shock of those fishermen.

KID: Go 'head, Looking Glass. You'll make some Apache an interesting wife.

LOOKING GLASS: And once I traveled to the South Pole.

PAT: South Pole.

LOOKING GLASS: Rather cold there.

PAT: Okay, Kate. This is how it is: I'm the sheriff... the law.

KID: Pat used to be with me… rustlin' cattle. We had fun, made money, and fell in love with all sorts of gals. Pretty girls love banditos.

PAT: Times are changing. Law is coming on strong. The Kid is part of the old ways: take a ride, carry a runnin' iron, change a few brands, and build a herd.

LOOKING GLASS: You're both thieves?

PAT: I'm reformed.

KID: I stay true to my nature.

PAT: I have a business opportunity. Government came to me…

KID: Government my backside. The business interests.

PAT: Government says to me, "Pat F. Garrett, if you go straight, we'll help you buy a ranch and stock it with slick Longhorns."

KID: What Pat means, Looking Glass, is the business interests will pay Pat to kill the best pal he ever had.

PAT: Billy, all I'm askin' is that you go off for three or four years. Take a holiday. Just get out of everybody's hair. You can come back someday. Heck, I'll cut you in on the profits.

LOOKING GLASS: (*To the* KID.) That deal sounds generous.

KID: Generous?

PAT: That's right, Kid. I get some fat cats helpin' me develop a ranch and all you have to do is ride that horse until you cool off.

KID: Looking Glass, I can't do that. It ain't honorable. (*Pause. Then to* LOOKING GLASS.) Here's a better plan: you partner-up with me. Take pictures of me ridin', rustlin', and shootin'. You're not hard to look at, girl, so I'll even take you dancin'.

PAT: Leave her out of this. She's a foundling sort of child.
LOOKING GLASS: I am seventeen. I will make my own decisions.

KID: See, Pat: she's seventeen. That's how old I was when the two of us started ridin' together. Looking Glass is a sign to me.

LOOKING GLASS: I'm not a damned sign.

KID: But you'll stick with me, right? You take the pictures and I'll write the true book about me.

PAT: Kid, leave it alone.

KID: Go collect your pay, Pat. Catch who you can. Stay off my trail.

PAT: I can't, Kid. It looks like we're headin' for bad times for us.

KID: Then pick your time for a finish-fight.

LOOKING GLASS: (*To* PAT.) You'd shoot a friend?

PAT: (*To* LOOKING GLASS, *but looking at the* KID.) Anybody can kill an enemy, but it takes sand to kill a friend-gone-wrong.

KID: Pat, you're bein' dreadful serious. What's a few cows between pals?

PAT: You ought to thank me, Kid. I won't let your enemies kill you. I'll do it. A friend should do the work.

KID: (*To* LOOKING GLASS). Pat wants to be famous. I get it now. He shoots Billy the Kid and maybe Pat Garrett gets to be governor of New Mexico.

LOOKING GLASS: (*To* PAT.) Who's going to know? How can you become famous shooting a nobody?

KID: Nobody? I keep tellin' you, Looking Glass. I'm a legend.

PAT: (*Starts to slow-walk backwards out of the camp.*) Adios, dear friend. I tried to reason with you. (PAT *exits.*)

KID: (*Shouts toward the exited* PAT.) You can't outdraw me, Pat! No man alive can outdraw Billy the Kid! (*Long pause.*) What-all's gonna replace me? What kind a country is this gonna be?

LOOKING GLASS: Sit down, Gordon, you'll wear out your boots.

KID: My goddamned name ain't Gordon.

LOOKING GLASS: It's just an expression. (*Pause.*) You got a sweetheart?

KID: Maybe I do.

LOOKING GLASS: Maybe you're available.

KID: Yeah... I might be between sweethearts. (*Pause.*) Why?

LOOKING GLASS: I got a vision.

KID: More soul travel stuff?

LOOKING GLASS: There's a flash of comet dust through my brain.

155

KID: Dust to dust.

LOOKING GLASS: My vision says you'll fall later this year... be killed near Fort Sumner.

KID: Not likely.

LOOKING GLASS: My visions don't lie.

KID: Like this here dime novel says, may a man say his prayers 'fore he meets me.

LOOKING GLASS: If you don't have a sweetheart, I'll write to Pat... and ask for your things. That's a promise.

(*The* KID *goes to* LOOKING GLASS, *takes her into his arms. They quickly kiss.*)

KID: Will you keep your promise.

LOOKING GLASS: (*Kisses him again.*) Yes.

KID: Surely?

LOOKING GLASS: Honor bright.

(*A sudden hard wind comes up. A tumbleweed blows through. They stand apart... gaze at each other.*)

LIGHTS RISE TO FULL-BRIGHT, SNAP TO BLACK:
<u>THE END</u>

Red Shuttleworth is a 2017 Tanne Foundation Award recipient. His *Woe to the Land Shadowing* won the 2016 Western Heritage Wrangler Award for Outstanding Poetry Book. A three-time winner of the Western Writers of America Spur Award for Poetry, Shuttleworth was named "Best Living Western Poet" in 2007 by *True West* magazine. His plays have been presented widely, including at State University of New York at Fredonia, Saddleback College, Sundance Playwrights Lab, and the Tony Award-winning Utah Shakespearean Festival.

www.ingramcontent.com/pod-product-compliance
Lightning Source LLC
LaVergne TN
LVHW051238080426
835513LV00016B/1649

9 780615 953311